UP ALL DAY

UP ALL DAY

Rebecca Weller

Mod By Dom ~ Australia

UP ALL DAY

The content of this book is for general information only. Each person's physical, emotional, and spiritual condition is unique. The story in this book is not intended to replace or interrupt the reader's relationship with a physician or other professional. Please consult your doctor for matters pertaining to your specific health concerns.

Some names and identifying details have been changed to protect the privacy of individuals.

Cover and Interior Design by Dominic Garczynski

ISBN: 9780994602336
Digital ISBN: 9780994602329

For anyone who has ever had a dream.
May it change you in a way you'll never forget.

And for my family, who have supported all of my crazy dreams, always

ONE

Nobody ever warned me about the dreams. In the beginning, the leap took longer. The overwhelming wave of relief wouldn't arrive a split-second later; instead leaving me reeling for an eternity while my mind raced and fumbled, desperate to connect the dots.

I had no idea that a single REM cycle could transport me back to the deepest, darkest parts of my psyche. I'd tremble for minutes that felt like hours after my eyes flew open, my heart racing; my stomach sick with dread and guilt.

It's okay, I reassured myself, willing my pulse to slow down. *It was a dream; just a dream.* I was home. I was safe. It wasn't me, and it wasn't real life.

Dominic, my love, was sleeping soundly beside me. Being careful not to wake him, I gently slipped from beneath the covers and tiptoed towards the door.

"Where you going?" he mumbled, his eyes still closed.

"Recording a pep talk," I whispered, heading for the study in my pyjamas.

Wiping sleep from my eyes, I sank into my desk chair and pulled myself towards the microphone. With a click, I started recording.

My voice sounded every bit as emotional and vulnerable as I felt, but I didn't care. I wanted to share every detail of this dream while I was still so raw and shaken.

The dream took place at a work Christmas party, not unlike so many I'd been to before. A warm summer's breeze swirled past the live band, and colourful lanterns glowed across the garden. Everyone else was drinking and dancing and laughing.

Resentment simmered inside me. The voice of the inner Beast was back and on the brink of a ferocious tantrum, stuck in an infinite loop: It's only one drink! *Why can't you have one? What's the big deal?*

In a swift act of misguided rebellion, I grabbed the closest cocktail and downed it in one. Then I drank another, and another, splashing them down my throat while my colleagues rallied around, cheering me on with hollers of, "*Woohoo,* the old Bex is back!"

Completely wrapped up in the excitement, I let

loose, bouncing around the party, determined to catch up to everyone else's tipsiness; hell bent on having *The Best Night Ever!*

Everyone else started slowing down. Maybe they'd had enough to drink, or simply knew the night was coming to an end.

People started to leave. No doubt concerned about the condition I was in, one of my colleagues called Dom and asked him to come and collect me. Dom was furious and I was in no state to care.

The dream came to a haunting end.

As I awoke, before my mind had a chance to unscramble itself, an icy sensation spread through my veins. *Oh God, how did I get home? Did I make a fool of myself? What must everyone think?*

Every one of the old, horrifying, familiar feelings came rushing back: shame, frustration, heartbreaking self-sabotage, and knowing I couldn't trust myself. But worst of all, blinding self-hatred. In that nanosecond, in my mind, I had ruined everything.

And yet, try as I might, I couldn't bring myself to despise the dreams. In a society that glamorised alcohol, receiving a blinding image of the truth; of who I no longer was, and who I no longer had to be, felt like a gift. Like a beautiful - if terrifying - reminder of a life I didn't want to go back to.

What day is it? I wondered, rubbing my eyes as I headed back to bed, pushing my brain to think. *Saturday.*

Gently, careful not to wake Dom again, I slipped

back beneath the covers.

I was clearly triggered by this upcoming trip, that's all.

Reaching into my bedside drawer, I found a notebook and jotted down a few ideas to work on during the upcoming week. I'd never worked harder in my entire life than I had this past year.

But I could do more, I assured myself, quietly placing the notebook back into the drawer. Staying busy was the key to busting through all of these scary milestones. Staying busy would keep me on track.

~

The first time I ever boarded a plane, I was nine years old and travelling with my Mum, sister, and Nanna on a family holiday to Bali. From our home in Perth, one of the most isolated cities in the world, Bali was closer than any other city in Australia.

I remember getting all dressed up for the trip in my favourite pink and white dress, deciding at the last minute to pair it with white, knee-high socks to cover the eczema on my legs that never seemed to heal. My first memory of ever stepping off a plane was one of feeling suffocated by the humidity in my long white socks. I didn't care, though, I still loved the experience.

The second time I flew was on a spontaneous family trip to Melbourne when I was fifteen, back when the airlines offered 'Mystery flights' designed to fill seats at the last minute. We were informed of the destination only a day before the flight and were thrilled, imagining the shopping opportunities in Melbourne would be totally worth the four hour flight each way. That trip was forever etched in my mind because it was so freakishly hot that day, the tar became soft and toffee-like on the roads. I was appalled when I crossed the street that my brand new, white sandals got all sticky with black mess.

The next time I flew, I was nineteen, and by then I'd well and truly fallen under the spell of alcohol. Every trip since had involved ridiculous amounts of it. There'd been copious drinks as I packed my bags the night before, in airport bars, and on the plane itself. There'd been forgotten items, sleeping through alarms, and hangovers descending in a truly hideous fashion half-way through the flight. There'd been tearful arguments with boyfriends, frantically running to departure gates as my name reverberated through the airport, and even throwing up in airport bathrooms once or twice. Until now.

"Something to drink?" a flight attendant asked, stopping to fuss with her tiny silk scarf, just as I'd started a battle of wits with the in-flight entertainment system at 35,000 feet. Butterflies flip-flopping in my stomach had made it impossible to read, and now a movie also appeared frustratingly out of reach. I pulled off my headphones, grateful for the distraction.

Dom gestured to me to go first. The now perfectly groomed attendant smiled at me. For a moment, I hesitated. It was only 11:00am, but that'd never stopped me before. On a regular Perth to Sydney flight, I'd have downed at least three white wines; more if I could get away with it.

"Sparkling water please," I chirped, settling back into my seat and feeling rather chuffed with myself. My first alcohol-free order on a plane, *done*.

I remember when the term *dry wedding* was enough to send me screaming for the hills, never mind a dry *holiday*. I'd been on a few mini breaks since I stopped drinking fifteen months earlier, but not a real trip, involving airplanes and luggage and stuff. Okay, so technically this was a business trip, but I was doing work I loved, so in a way it felt like a holiday too.

"Thank you," I smiled as the attendant passed me a plastic cup of ice and a tiny can of sparkling water.

Look at me go! I thought to myself, taking a sip and feeling incredibly grown up. This time I wouldn't be fooling myself into thinking I was having a great time because I had an artificial buzz on. I was going to soak up every magical second of this experience; nerves, excitement and all.

Wriggling around so I could reach the tote bag I'd stowed under the seat in front of me, I pulled out my journal and a pen. Writing calmed me. It always had. It didn't really matter what I wrote; just the physical act of writing anything at all seemed to have a comforting effect.

I especially loved writing on planes. There was something so weird and uniquely wonderful about a large crowd of people all sitting quietly in their seats - *if you were lucky* - this high in the sky. Being together with people but essentially in your own little bubble always sparked my creativity somehow. Like all the emails and social media messages and spreadsheets and deadlines were being taken care of down there on Earth somewhere, while I was left free to dream in the sky.

Okay, so the cabin was often cramped and stuffy, and I always prayed I wouldn't be seated next to someone who last took a shower during Halley's Comet, or in front of a kid who made it his personal game to kick the stuffing out of the back of my seat. But one look out the window at the infinite blue expanse of sky and the billowy white clouds below, and I'd see possibility where there was none before. I'd become excited about new ideas and the magic of *making things happen.*

And *oh,* was I excited about this idea. I craved it. We'd been working our butts off when the invitation arrived, running four different websites, which kind of felt like having four babies in four different houses. Constantly running from one to another; constantly feeling like you were letting every one of them down.

The great irony of running a wellness coaching business, it seemed, was helping people with self-care every day while having little time for it myself. We really didn't have the time, energy or budget to fly across the country to attend a single workshop, but I knew we needed this trip to breathe fresh life back into us and our work. To renew my inspiration, not only for what I could create to help others, but for my very sobriety.

~

Goosebumps tickled their way up and down my arms as I reached into my bag to double-check I still had my notebook. "*Pinch me!,*" I joked, sneaking a sideways glance at Dom.

"Geek!" he said, making a big show of adjusting his novelty spaceman belt.

The automatic double doors swung open before us in a dramatic fashion. Taking a deep breath, I pulled my shoulders back, channelling those movie scenes I'd always loved where people swagger through the room in slow motion. There was no going back now.

My inner nerd had always wanted to see the inside of a super tech company. The reception area was just as I'd imagined. An exceptionally long, shiny reception desk was lit up at multiple angles by ultra-sleek light fittings, while lush indoor plants sprang precariously from the walls. It also felt surprisingly fun to be back in a real office for the first time in two years.

"Hello," the receptionist smiled.

"Hi, um, we're here for the event?" I managed, while Dom told her our full names. The receptionist nodded, printing our Visitor ID badges and directing us to the lifts that would take us to the second floor.

"*Eeeep,* it's so cool," I whispered to Dom, barely able to stop myself from skipping along like an animated toddler.

"*Shhh.*" He winked, pressing a finger to his lips.

The lift area was decorated like an underground train station; even down to the lift doors resembling those on a train. As we approached, the closest doors slid open as if they'd always been waiting for us. As we stepped inside, a man ran in to join us, making it just in time before the doors closed. Wearing a satchel bag and carrying a scooter that effortlessly folded up in his hands, he had that undeniable school-geek turned too-cool-for-school air of someone who worked there. As he got out at the first floor, I wondered what it must be like to work in a place like this every day.

On the second floor, we followed temporary sign posts that directed us to a large waiting area. The walls nearby were alive with installations. One side was decorated with graffiti art depicting cartoon characters and funny captions. Another was decorated almost entirely with stacked milk crates.

Several large, round sofa seats filled the space and we plopped down on one of them, content to people-watch while we waited. A dozen or so people milled around the room, snapping photos and videos on their phones.

Dom gave me a little nudge. "Shall we take a photo?"

"Later," I told him. "I don't want to miss a thing."

As if on cue, the doors to a nearby room swung open and a tanned, pony-tail wearing man appeared. "Welcome, everyone!" he boomed. "Come in; find a seat."

Dom and I headed in to choose a table towards the back of the room. I may have been excited to be there, but I wasn't quite ready to risk being called on in front of such a large group.

"Recognise anyone?" Dom leaned over to whisper. The room held fifty or so seats that were filling up fast.

"Those two," I whispered, nodding towards two women who'd just walked in. "They're sisters who run a popular wellness website together. But no one else so far."

The man who welcomed us into the room stood at the front before two large projector screens. He waited for the excited chatter to die down before speaking.

"Welcome, everyone, to the first ever gathering of Australia's top health and fitness industry leaders. You were invited to this workshop because we see potential in you; in the stories and videos you're creating."

Fitness?, my mind echoed. I squirmed in my seat, feeling like an imposter. What if they'd sent me the invitation by mistake? I mean, I wasn't a fitness bunny or anything.

Oh my God. What if I was the most unfit person in the room? Would they take one look at me and know that

I couldn't do cross-fit, or chin-ups, or burpees, or whatever the heck they were called, and boot-camp me the hell out of here?

Dom looked over at me and grinned, clearly amused by the look on my face.

I pulled awkwardly at my blazer. The dress code for this event had been frustratingly unclear. I'd finally settled on jeans, a smart blouse and a blazer, thinking that would at least cover all bases: simple, not too casual, not too corporate.

Looking around again, I saw that most of the other attendees wore jeans and jumpers. *Phew, no activewear or obvious muscles on display, then.*

Exhaling, I tried to focus on what the host was saying. The invitation had mentioned networking drinks after the workshop. I'd never been a big fan of networking events, not even when I was drinking. The small talk about what you did, how long you'd done it for, and which department you did it in, always drove me bonkers. I'd avoided them as much as possible, regardless of whether free drinks had been involved.

But now I craved connection. Working from home was fun at first, but once the novelty wore off it felt quite lonely at times. I loved having Dom to work with but I also missed having other colleagues to laugh with over coffee breaks. Missed it so much, in fact, that I'd even begun to romanticise all those long, pointless meetings that previously drove me nuts, and randomly chatting about the weather at the water cooler, or bonding over the photocopier being jammed.

"Thank you so much, everyone," the host called from the front of the room. I glanced at the large wall clock behind him and was shocked to see it was already five o'clock. "If you'd like to move out into the main room, we have refreshments waiting for you."

"Here goes," I whispered to Dom as we followed the crowd. I flicked my right wrist, trying to alleviate a cramp from writing pages of notes. Dom reached over to give my hand a playful squeeze.

Focus on the good stuff, I reminded myself. Concentrating on the atmosphere, food, venue and conversations was one of the strategies that usually helped to keep my nerves at bay and make sober socialising easier. *Plus, we can always leave early if we want to,* I reassured myself.

Out in the main room, a long bench had been transformed into a grazing table. Another table nearby was lined with dozens of glasses of wine and bottles of beer. I couldn't yet spot any alcohol-free drinks.

"Maybe we just grab them from the fridge?" Dom suggested, pointing to the wall on the other side of the room that was lined with glass-doored fridges.

"Let's do it," I agreed as we manoeuvred our way through the crowd.

Once we'd each poured ourselves a glass of sparking water, we were fresh out of procrastination excuses. We shuffled our way over to a small group of people who were chatting nearby.

"Hi!" one of the women exclaimed, turning towards me. "I'm Elena."

"Hi," I beamed. "I'm Rebecca, and this is my partner, in business and love, Dominic."

"Oh you work together!" she smiled. "What do you do?"

"Uh, well, a few things actually," I stalled, while my mind scrambled to find the file marked 'Elevator Pitch'. "We started with a wellness website, where I share recipes and help women to have more energy. I think that's what earned us the invitation to be here," I paused, waving vaguely around the room. She waited for me to go on. "I also help other coaches with their businesses. And we have an online sobriety program where I help women to live alcohol-free," I smiled, relieved to have gotten it all out in a semi-coherent manner.

"Sobriety?" She said, her face changing slightly; her lips pursing into a thin line. She glanced down at the glass of wine in her hand.

"Uh-huh," I nodded.

"Oh," she said. "And how did you get into that?"

"It was actually through my own personal journey," I said vaguely, sensing her discomfort and wanting to change the subject as quickly as possible. "So how about you? What do you do?"

Elena briefly shared a little about her company before nudging her colleague. "Okay, well it was nice to meet you. We're going to keep mingling." Before I had a chance to respond, she waved and dragged her colleague away.

"Bye," I said, deflated. I'd always suspected net-working events might be weird now that I was a non-drinker. I'd never stopped to consider that it might also be difficult to tell people what I did when they had a drink in their hand.

"Awkward," I whispered to Dom.

"*Aaahh,* it's fine," he shrugged. "Let's try again."

A couple of men were chatting nearby and we moved over to join their conversation, just as they drifted off to talk to other people.

I fidgeted nervously. "Maybe we just chat amongst ourselves for a while?"

"Good idea," Dom said. "What was your favour-ite lesson from today?"

I giggled. "Thank goodness for the internet; it's an introvert's paradise?"

Dom laughed. "Come on, chuckles, let's go try again."

Two more conversation hops and I was done.

"Let's go," I said to Dom.

"Really? I figured we've come all this way, we should stay to the end."

The old me would have given anything to hear him say that. The old me didn't live here anymore.

"I've had enough," I said. "Shall we get some dinner?"

"Sure," he smiled, taking my hand and leading the way.

Out on the street, we flagged down a taxi. As the

car pulled away from the kerb, I still couldn't shake feeling deflated. *Give it time,* I reminded myself, as Dom chatted to the driver. *It was just your first time.*

I had to admit that nerves and awkwardness were still a hell of a lot better than my old standard mode of operation. How many work events in the past had left me feeling sick with dread, desperately trying to remember what I did or said; queasy with anxiety over what my colleagues would say on Monday morning?

It wasn't until the flight home the next day that I made the rookie mistake of scrolling through social media. As I came across photos of our peers who'd stayed longer that night, I felt a deep, gnawing pang of missing out. They posed across reception desks, holding up props, making funny faces, and looking like they were having a whale of a time.

I shook my head, snapping myself out of it. Of course it was going to feel a little strange not being the last to leave the party. But these photos weren't the whole story; they were just the highlight reel. Who knows what sore and sorry heads surfaced the following morning.

With a nod, I switched off my phone and settled back into my seat, attempting to steer my mind in an entirely different direction. The sun had begun to set beyond my window, and I closed my eyes, leaning into its warmth, willing this plane to hurry up and take off already.

TWO

I don't remember ever being great with numbers. In High School, while I did well in subjects like History and English Literature, Mathematics was always the class I dreaded most. I wasn't too concerned that I was terrible at it. I had no idea what I wanted to do with my life, and therefore no concrete plans to ever use it for anything anyway.

There was only one thing I'd ever really wanted to do, and that was to write. While I was fairly sure I lacked the killer instincts required to be a journalist, when it came time to apply to university, I wrote journalism down anyway. Never having truly applied myself, it turned out the 'killer instinct' part was besides the point. I lacked the grades required to compete against all the other budding journalists in the state.

More embarrassed than crushed when the rejection letters arrived, I decided to try a different route. That summer I spent weeks trawling through newspapers, writing and sending off applications for junior traineeship positions in fields like media, communications and public relations. Basically, any position that sounded remotely like it might someday involve some kind of writing.

My first interview was at a marketing company. The manager was a confident, charismatic man who smiled as I sat on the other side of his large, gleaming desk, and boomed, "So, Rebecca! Tell me! What are you *passionate* about?"

As a shy seventeen-year-old with zero self-awareness and even less life direction, I was completely baffled by this question, and thought this must be some strange 'marketing speak' I wasn't privy to. I mumbled something about being passionate about "my life" but honestly, I didn't have a clue.

Watching the smile fade from behind his eyes was an extraordinary form of torture, and walking out of that room I felt the suffocating weight of his disappointment. Needless to say, I didn't get the job.

My next interview was at a brand agency that was notorious around the city for hiring only the highest calibre of talent. Shocked to have even secured a meeting, I spent hours fussing over just the right outfit, determined to look the part; convinced this would score me the position.

The office building was stylish and beautiful, and as I was called into the boardroom, I felt like I'd finally found my future.

A man and a woman sat on one side of the large boardroom table. I was encouraged to see their faces light up as I entered.

"Please, take a seat," the man smiled, introducing them both while he gestured for me to sit opposite them.

"So, Rebecca," he said, leaning forwards slightly. "We were very impressed with your application. We received hundreds for the position and yours stood out immediately."

I beamed. Finally, *finally*, this was it. I was on my way to that vague office/writing job I'd always dreamed of.

"So tell us," he said, sharing a sideways look of anticipation with his colleague before continuing. "What made you submit your application in a coloured envelope?"

I blinked at him, not understanding the question. I looked at the woman for clues. They both stared at me, waiting for my answer. Every ounce of their hope and expectation radiated across the table; that I was the one they'd been looking for.

Flustered and racking my brain, I glanced down at the table. There, in the manila folder in front of him, I saw it: the bright red envelope I'd sent simply because I'd applied for so many jobs that I'd used up all of my white ones. In desperation, wanting to get my application into the post before the deadline, I'd searched my childhood writing sets for anything I could possibly use.

For years afterwards I'd kick myself for not thinking faster and telling them what they wanted to hear: that I'd chosen that red envelope because I knew precisely what it took to stand out in a crowded market. Instead, ever the shy and awkward teenager, I'd mumbled my way through the truth.

Once again, I felt truly mortified as the smiles faded from behind their eyes. Once again, I walked out of the room drenched in their disappointment, and feeling every inch the loser.

It didn't take many more interviews like this to find myself enrolling to study Business Administration and Accounting at technical college, and thoroughly struggling with the accounting part.

~

"Ugh! Let's take a break," I grumbled, massaging my temples. Since Dom and I had launched into business for ourselves two years earlier, I felt like I'd never analysed numbers so closely in my life. We couldn't yet afford to hire a bookkeeper so it was my responsibility to complete our company tax reports every quarter. I hated every second of it, but I was grateful that at least my accidental background in finance meant I could almost understand it. It was only 9:00am and I was still knee deep in preparing our reports, but I needed to get out. I was starting to feel the walls closing in.

Dom was working at his desk in the living room that also doubled as our dining table. "Coffee and cake?" I suggested, doing a silly little dance designed to make him laugh. His cheeks revealed the most amazing dimples when he laughed and I never grew tired of seeing them.

Without skipping a beat, he grinned and jumped up to grab his cap from the bedroom. "Let's go."

Our regular stress management walks around the neighbourhood usually took us to one of two places: the post office or our favourite cafe. On this challenging morning filled with reporting headaches, I decided we needed both.

The cafe was located just a few streets away from our apartment, and in the rear of a dress shop, which always made me feel nostalgic about a time when department stores had their own cafes. There was probably nothing all that wonderful about that, and yet for some reason I had the warmest memories of my sister and I loading up plastic trays with buckets of hot chips and cups of jelly and custard.

The cafe was fairly busy when we arrived, the walls echoing with chatter and the occasional hiss of an espresso machine as we waited to place our orders.

"Hi guys!" our favourite barista, Melissa, called out as she spotted us from behind the machine. "Just give us a sec."

"I'm here, hello hello!" the cafe owner, Gaye, sang out as she bustled in carrying a stack of empty plates. "You're just in time." Setting the plates down, she wiped her hands on her apron and waved her hands in front of a nearby display case. "Ta-da! Try some of this. It's a new recipe."

Gaye made the most scrumptious cakes, cooked in a rice cooker, no less. She was warm and quirky and loved to fuss over us as though she was our Mother. I adored her.

Pulling out the cake and cutting us each a sliver, she handed it to us to try.

"Yep!" Dom said, barely swallowing before getting the words out. "Two please, with cappuccinos."

"Coming right up!" Gaye smiled, as we searched the cafe for a seat.

"Okay," I said, ready to get down to business as soon as we'd settled into a cosy little wooden table in the corner. "So once I've finished these financial reports, I'll start work on my client notes. But also, I had an idea!" I paused for dramatic effect. "What if… we created an online academy kind of thing and put all of our courses into it? Like the free class with lessons from the trip, and any other classes we dream up. And maybe even our wellness courses too?"

Dom nodded slowly and looked a little weary. "I like it," he said, rubbing his forehead like he was wishing away a headache. "I see how it could help simplify things. But do you think we should have a bit of a rest first?"

"We can't!" I said, panicked that he might even consider that. "We've got too much to do."

"Okay," he nodded, sitting up straighter in his chair. "What's next? Did you send your final wellness newsletter?"

"Well, no…" I said, scrambling to explain as Dom opened his mouth to protest. "It's just that I have a couple of last things I want to send the guys on that list. They've been with me from the start and I want to make sure they feel loved before I close it down."

Dom took a bite of his cake, and then sighed. "You can't do it all. I thought we agreed that business and sobriety coaching would be your focus going forward."

"I know," I said, running my finger along a groove on the table. "It's just that I want to help them all."

"It's someone else's turn to help them with that now," Dom said. "Come on, let's go see if there's anything waiting for us in the post box."

The post office was just a few streets away, and I relished the fresh air on my face as we walked. We'd originally settled on this neighbourhood because it was located halfway between our two offices when we were in the corporate world, and I'd always loved the energy on these streets. People rushed by carrying takeaway coffees and laptop bags, and making terribly important phone calls. The buzz of it always made me feel more energised in work and creativity.

As we reached our post box and unlocked the door, I was thrilled to discover a parcel inside, postmarked from the USA. Delighted, I flipped the envelope over.

"It's from Amy!" I gasped, seeing the sticker with her name.

Amy was a blogger I'd met four years earlier. We'd swapped recipes and tips and cheered each other on as our little blogs had grown.

I tore the parcel open with excitement. It was a copy of Amy's very first book. I ran my fingers over her name on the front cover, giddy with excitement and pride for her, imagining how it must have felt to see her own name in print for the first time.

Months earlier, Amy had invited her food blogger friends to contribute a recipe each to her book. Flipping through the pages, I gasped as I found it. Page 117: Bex's Eggplant Chana Masala. I'd seen my name and work in print in several magazines and newspapers since I'd started this crazy entrepreneurial journey, but never in a book. Not until now. They were just tiny words printed on a page and yet somehow they took my breath away. Suddenly overcome with emotion, I wondered if I might cry.

Many of my beautiful readers and subscribers had asked me to create a cookbook over the years. While it was a fun idea to think about, it'd never felt quite right to me. Like I'd be stepping into someone else's shoes. Someone else's dream, maybe.

Deep down I'd always had a vision of someday

publishing a written book; a novel. I had no clue what it would be about, but to create anything else just wouldn't feel like my dream.

"So amazing," I beamed at Dom as we turned to walk back home. I couldn't wait to ask Amy what it felt like to be a real, live Author.

"Oh, and great news!" Dom said, interrupting my train of thought a few minutes later as he turned the key in our front door. "Ben's offered us his apartment to film in next Friday while he's at work."

"Oh wow!" Our friend Ben lived in a high-rise apartment in the city, with sweeping views across the river. It would be the perfect place to film the videos for Dom's new course. "So we can escape the noise?"

"Yep, and have a change of scene as a backdrop, so that my videos are slightly different to yours. He's planning on having some friends over that night so the place will be super clean and tidy."

"Oh," I said, crestfallen, wondering if maybe non-drinkers weren't invited. "Some friends...? But not us?"

"Of course us too, silly!" Dom laughed, ushering me through the door.

~

Ben had moved into his apartment so recently that I hadn't yet had a chance to see it.

"This way," Dom said, following the signs as we got out of the lift, leading us down a long corridor before stopping next to one of the doors. "It's this one." Turning the key in the lock, he swung the door open, revealing a large, modern apartment on the 26th floor.

"It's so quiet," I whispered, walking straight through the kitchen and living room to reach the large balcony window.

"It's surprisingly peaceful." Dom closed the front door behind him and joined me at the window. The view was spectacular. In the park below, we could see people playing soccer. Sunlight sparkled across the river, while small boats cruised past.

We were right in the centre of the city and yet the traffic noise was barely a low hum at this height; a tiny squeak compared to the lion's roar of drills and jack-hammers we heard every day in our own apartment.

It had been almost three years since Dom and I had moved into our first home together. We were so excited then; so full of hope for our new abode. Our city had been in the midst of a crazy property boom that had sent the rental market skyrocketing, and we couldn't believe our luck at being able to secure a property at all, never mind at a relatively affordable price.

The very next week, a construction crew arrived. With them came large expanses of scaffolding, an impossibly huge crane, and all the machinery required to build a new apartment complex right next door.

For the first six months we were still working in the corporate world, so it didn't bother us much. The crew started work at 7:00am, but we were both up by then and usually off to our offices. But when we both began working from home, it quickly became challenging, forcing us to schedule client calls and video recording around the construction crew's schedule. All day long we wore noise-cancelling headphones, and at night we enjoyed the sweet relief of silence.

Having the opportunity to work from Ben's apartment for the day, especially when we were under pressure to finish filming videos for a new course we were putting together, was a dream come true.

"Okay, where shall we set up?" I asked Dom as I unpacked the tripod.

"*Hhmmm*," Dom mused, turning slowly to take in the whole living room. "Let's start over on this couch and see how it looks."

"Roger that!" I saluted, helping him to set up the camera and lighting equipment.

Thankfully I'd already finished filming my videos the previous Sunday when the construction crew were away. I was looking forward to taking a bit of a breather.

As Dom started filming, I quietly let myself out onto the balcony. My friend Zara had recently bought an apartment in this neighbourhood. I peered at the nearby balconies, one by one, wondering which one was hers and what it would be like to live here with this amazing view.

Zara and I had last caught up at a cafe a couple of weeks earlier, just before she'd moved. I'd expected a relaxed chat and laugh, but at one point she'd gotten all serious.

"How's everything going with you?" she asked, stirring a straw into her smoothie, watching me with a look I couldn't quite read. Before I had a chance to answer, she continued. "I've been a bit worried about you lately, seeing how much content you've been pumping out."

Caught off guard, I'd confessed that I was probably overdoing it a bit. But I assured her that it was only temporary; that sooner or later, all the balls would be in the air and would stay there.

As the glare of sunshine reflected back from one of the balconies, I smiled, excited to tell her about my new idea to create an academy. This would be the answer to helping more people while not burning out, I was sure of it.

The wind was starting to pick up on the balcony so I wandered back into the living room to find Dom still filming. As silently as possible, I pulled a notebook and pen from my bag and wandered down to the small office at the back of the apartment. The window faced the same direction as the balcony, and I sat staring out at the view, giving myself permission to just sit and daydream for a few minutes. It felt like an age since I'd last done that.

Eventually I opened my notebook. I'd been invited to speak at an event that was fast approaching and I still had an entire presentation to come up with. I bit the end of my pen, considering possible topics and trying not to get too freaked out about the whole thing.

I'd been working on the presentation for a couple of hours when I heard a key in the door. Thrilled to take a break, I hurried out to the living room to greet Ben.

"You're home!" I cheered, hugging him. "This place is amazing. Thank you so much for lending it to us."

"My pleasure," Ben said with a smile. "Did you finish your videos?"

"I think so," Dom said, coming in from the living room. "I'll check the footage in a minute, but did you want a hand setting up?"

"Nah, it's all good," Ben said. "Go check your stuff. I've got this."

"And I can help," I said. "What's first?"

"Great," Ben said, clapping his hands together before pointing behind me. "Do you want to pull a couple of bowls out of that cupboard there?"

"Sure thing," I said, bringing them over to the kitchen bench and plopping myself down on a stool.

"So how's things with you guys?" Ben asked as he started unpacking a grocery bag onto the counter. "Dom said you're doing a book course or something?"

"Huh?" I said, momentarily confused; my head still full of presentation ideas. "Oh yeah!" I said as it finally clicked. "The school where I studied health coaching offered me a place in their new book course."

"Cool," he said, unwrapping various cheeses and

arranging them on a platter. "What will the book be about?"

"Well, it's not a concrete plan or anything yet." I said, waving the question away, my face and neck curiously hot all of a sudden. "I'm grateful for the gift, but we really don't have time for a book right now. I figured I could just attend the classes and save the info for later."

"Oh," he said, giving me a funny look, before returning to rummage in the fridge and emerging with a bowl of olives. "It sounds like you guys have been pretty busy lately?"

"Uh-huh," I rolled my eyes and laughed. We were still pulling twelve to fourteen hour days, so 'pretty busy' felt like the understatement of the century. "But it's just temporary," I assured him.

Ben opened a packet of crackers and emptied them onto a plate. "If you wrote one later, what would it would be about?"

"Well, that's the fifty-million dollar question," I admitted. "Many of our members have asked me to share more of my personal story. I guess they want to know what my early sobriety was like and that I struggled with the same things as them too. And I do like that idea. It's just a bit scary, I guess."

"How so?"

"I don't know," I shrugged. Ben was quite possibly the most confident human I'd ever met and I wasn't entirely sure he'd understand. "Maybe because - " The intercom buzzed and I'd never felt more relieved to be cut off mid-sentence in my life.

"Hey mate, come on up," Ben barked into the intercom, before heading over to open the front door.

In any case, it's not just fear holding me back, I reassured myself. I couldn't possibly fit one more thing into my schedule and I refused to feel guilty or bad about that. Even if I'd wanted to attempt another project right now, there was no way I had the time. The whole idea was preposterous.

Ben's friends walked through the front door and I jumped up to greet them, grateful to escape the topic.

There was just one little problem, of course. Living a sober life meant having nowhere to hide.

THREE

For months, whenever I'd thought of this event date, my stomach lurched. I'd hosted my own small events before, but I'd never spoken at someone else's. This would be my longest talk so far, in front of the largest audience. But scariest of all, it would be the first time I'd speak publicly about my drinking past.

Look up any list of common human fears and you'll find public speaking at the top. It doesn't matter if our message is important and helpful, or if we're excited to share it, for the vast majority of humans, the prospect is still terrifying. Times that by ten for humans who'd spent the past twenty-odd years successfully convincing themselves they were born extroverts, only to be reunited in sobriety with the introverted soul they'd always possessed.

I stood in front of my wardrobe, still completely torn about what to wear. Without Dutch Courage to hide behind, I usually felt more confident at events if I wore something I loved; something that made me happy. Sometimes it was a new dress that gave me that little boost I needed to get through the doors; sometimes it was my favourite earrings or lipstick.

My friend Sophie's words ricocheted around my head: "For that kind of venue and event, don't dress too nicely. You don't want to seem like you're unrelatable."

I could already feel the warmth of the early Summer's day, and I worried I wouldn't be able to strike the right balance between warm and cool; professional and personable. I closed my eyes and visualised like mad, imagining myself on stage feeling happy, confident - and precisely the right temperature. *What would that woman wear?*

A flurry of butterflies wreaked havoc in my stomach and chest, my mind alternating between incredible excitement, and wanting to run a mile.

"Ugh!" I groaned out loud, opening my eyes. My gaze fell to a navy and white striped t-shirt, jeans, and ballet flats. Perfect. If I turned out to be underdressed, heck, at least I'd be comfortable.

I dressed quickly and headed to my desk to check that my presentation was ready. I'd labelled my presentation notes: 'My Super Exciting Talk at the Perth

Vegan Festival' in an attempt to convince my subconscious that this was fun rather than petrifying.

Dom popped his head around the doorframe. "Ready?"

I took a deep breath. "Uh huh," I nodded.

He looked me up and down. "No heels? I thought you said they made you feel powerful?"

"Yeah," I nodded. "I also feel powerful when I don't fall on my face."

"*Aaahh,*" he smiled and nodded.

"Actually, you know what?" I said, changing my mind. "I'll take a pair of heels too, and just decide when we get there."

Dom opened his mouth to say something but clearly thought better of it, and left me to it. I grabbed a large bag from my cupboard and tucked a pair of heels and a cardigan inside, along with my notes and the thumb drive that held my presentation slides. In the kitchen, I grabbed a bottle of water, a packet of peppermints, and a tiny bottle of essential oils.

"Okay, let's do this!" I called out to Dom, heading for the front door.

"It's going to be great," Dom said. "*You'll* be great."

I tried to smile but was fairly certain it came out as a grimace. "I hope so."

The bus lurched forward as the driver did a late braking manoeuvre, narrowly stopping for a red light. I grabbed the railing in front of us and glanced at Dom. Thank heavens we'd been able to find a seat. Since our little hatchback had just turned sixteen years old and appeared to be firmly in the 'temperamental teenager' stage, catching the city-link bus had seemed like a much better idea. The car was too unreliable to count on to get us anywhere on time, and the event venue was only a few minutes ride away. Although, my stomach was now having second thoughts.

I took another deep, shaky breath in an attempt to dispel my nerves, and looked out the window just in time to notice that we were passing my old work building. A few years earlier, my then-boss had asked if I'd like to give a presentation at our next large monthly meeting.

"No way!" I'd scoffed as he'd looked at me strangely. It was only in hindsight that I realised it probably wasn't the best career move, but the truth of the matter was that I couldn't think of anything worse. I could barely utter two sentences in those meetings without shivering and shaking all over the place, never mind standing at the podium to give an entire presentation. And that presentation was only about financial stuff! Here I was, about to share my own, very personal story with a room full of strangers. My stomach flipped violently and I prayed we'd get there soon. It suddenly felt suffocating on this bus.

I opened my little bottle of essential oils and

attempted to wave it under my nostrils. It was a calming blend that my friend Diana had assured me would relax even the biggest anxieties. The bus lurched again, and I succeeded only in splashing it down my chin. Dom closed his eyes and shook his head at my ridiculousness, while I rummaged around in my bag for a tissue. *How elegant and lady-like,* I thought to myself wryly.

Thankfully the next stop was ours. As we grabbed our things and clambered off the bus, I felt marginally better. I'd wanted to challenge myself to do this, even if it was a roaring disaster, because of how it might *change* me, just as sobriety had. Okay, so public speaking had always been one of my biggest fears in the corporate world, but I was a different person now. I'd found the courage to stop drinking, and to accept this invitation. Now I really wanted to prove to myself that I could do this. Plus, the entire invitation had felt like kismet.

"This is it," I said, pointing to the nightclub entrance.

Dom looked at the area I was pointing to, taking in the grungy double doors and blackened windows covered in posters advertising upcoming gigs. His brow crinkled. "Are you sure?"

"Oh, I'm sure," I nodded, pushing open one of the doors.

In the small, dimly lit lobby, a woman sat in a ticket booth. She appeared to be in her twenties and was dressed all in black with black painted nails. Tattoos covered both of her arms.

"Hi," I smiled, feeling grateful that I'd dressed down, although perhaps a tad conservatively by comparison. The woman looked at me and waited for me to go on. "Uh, my name's Rebecca Weller and I'm one of the speakers?"

She looked at a chart and then nodded. Reaching out and grabbing my hand, she pulled my arm closer so she could stamp the inside of my wrist. She motioned to Dom that he should do the same and he complied, gazing at his stamp in amusement.

"Zach's inside somewhere," the woman said. "Maybe up at the back stage."

"Okay," I nodded, hoping I'd be able to find him before I was due to go on. I had no idea what Zach looked like, or anything about him really besides the fact that he had hosted several events around the country with his wife. They were heavily into the music scene, which was presumably why they'd chosen a nightclub for a vegan festival that took place at noon on a Sunday, rather than say, a sunny park or garden.

We hadn't rehearsed or anything, and Zach hadn't given me a run sheet. In fact, besides a quick email invitation, I hadn't received any instruction whatsoever.

Don't be such a control freak, I chided myself. *Be cool.*

"This way," I motioned to Dom, pushing open a nearby door. After the bright midday sun outside, the nightclub appeared pitch black. Not that it mattered. I knew exactly where I was going. I reached out for Dom's hand to guide him.

If I remembered correctly, the main stage was just around the next bend. Sure enough, in a few more steps we reached the main room. A woman's voice was amplified from the large stage at the back of the room, and it sounded as though she was doing a cooking demonstration. As we approached, I could almost make her out amongst the bright lights and the throngs of people standing behind many rows of chairs.

I smiled at Dom through the darkness as our shoes began to stick to the floor. The club smelled like stale beer and cider, and faintly, like vomit. It felt a world away from the gorgeous day outside, or any of the high vibration places I'd been hanging out in for the past year or so.

I squeezed Dom's hand and led him through the doorway at the back of the room. Walking past the ladies bathroom, I shook my head at the perfect irony of it all, everything still in the same place after all these years.

I hadn't been inside a nightclub since I'd stopped drinking, but this was one I was very familiar with. I'd been there many times in my early party days. Once, when I was nineteen, my friends and I had gotten drunk, knocking back cheap blue cocktails because it was *Ladies Night.*

The next thing I remember was waking up in

a bathroom stall. Unfamiliar noises reverberated from the club. Staggering out, I discovered all of the house lights switched on, and the loud whir of cleaning machines running across the floors. Sunlight streamed in through the open front doors. My friends were long gone.

Dazed and confused, I began the walk of shame home. It was a ritual that became all too familiar over the following years.

And now here I was, more than twenty years later, more than twenty months sober, invited to share what I'd learnt about wellness and vitality, in the exact same venue.

The smaller room housed a smaller stage. From what I could gather, this was the stage I'd be speaking on. It was currently empty and all the house lights were turned on. People milled in and out of the back doors where dozens of food stalls served all kinds of vegan dishes and drinks. Small shards of light bounced across the hundreds of compact disks hanging from the ceiling. Posters lined the walls, and rows of chairs were lined before the stage. I imagined the chairs filled with people and my stomach did a massive somersault.

"Let's sit here for a sec," I said to Dom, pointing towards a couple of chairs in the back. "I just want to take it all in."

"Okay," Dom nodded, while I pulled out my little bottle of essential oils again. There was still an hour until my talk was due to begin; plenty of time to get my breathing and heart rate under control.

I'd just managed to inhale deeply a few times when a man leapt onto the stage to introduce a speaker. I reached out and squeezed Dom's hand, thrilled to be able to watch a talk from start to finish. As the stage lights came on and the house lights dimmed, a few people wandered in from outdoors to sit down and watch, but most continued milling about, chatting, eating and moving from one room to another.

I once read an article that said the mental health of flight attendants was impacted because passengers didn't listen to them as they explained the safety procedures. I'd been sure to give all attendants my full eye contact ever since.

I watched the speaker now to see if she was bothered by the people not listening, but I couldn't tell. Her voice and hands had been visibly shaking since she started her talk. Come to think of it, the voice of the woman in the other room had been shaking too.

"I think the speakers are nervous!" I whispered to Dom.

"Yeah," he shrugged and nodded. "Most people would be."

I sat back in my seat, wide-eyed. How incredible. I was convinced that the others would be seasoned professionals and a hard act to follow. How magnificent to discover we were all in the same boat.

And actually, the more I thought about it, the more I quite liked the fact that there was no formal audience in this room; that people sat down for a moment or two to eat their food, and then moved on. Thank goodness we'd arrived early. Now I could prepare myself for the same thing during my talk and understand that it wasn't personal. It wasn't that my talk was boring; it was just the culture in this room. Not having to keep a captive audience enthralled really took the pressure off.

I felt my body relax a little. Just then, my phone buzzed. It was a text message from my friend Lily, "We're here!"

"In the back room," I texted back, grinning. Lily and I had met and bonded at my last job many years prior and we'd been close friends ever since. I'd sent her a free ticket earlier that the organisers had emailed me and I was thrilled she'd made it in time for my talk.

We spotted her as she walked in with her love, Matt, and waved them over, silently motioning that they should sit with us. The talk ended a few minutes later, and we all gave the speaker a big round of applause.

"Hi honeys!" I squealed, reaching over to give them each a hug. "Thank you for coming."

"Have you guys eaten yet?" Lily asked. "Do we have time?"

I checked my phone. I still had twenty minutes until my talk was due to start but there was still no sign of Zach.

"Uh," I said, looking around the room to see if I could spot anyone who might be him. "Let me just see if I can find the organiser. You guys go ahead and we'll come find you."

"Sounds great," Lily said as she and Matt headed for the food stalls out the back.

I continued scanning the room, still not seeing anyone who might be him. "He's gotta be around here somewhere."

"What if we ask the sound guy?" Dom suggested, pointing towards the stage where a technician was moving microphones around and adjusting equipment. "I'll need to give him the presentation anyway."

"Let's do it," I nodded, acting braver than I felt.

The sound technician was busily wrapping cables around his arm in a large circle as we approached.

"Hi," I said. "I'm Rebecca Weller and I think I'm on next?"

"Great," he said. "Do you have your presentation?"

"I've got it," Dom said, producing a memory stick. "Shall we do a test run on your computer and make sure it's working okay?"

The technician nodded, signalling that Dom should follow him to the laptop. I took the chance to pull my notes out of my bag and gave them another read through.

"Okay, all done," Dom said, coming back over. "Let's go find the others."

Fabulous. I loved the idea of mixing with the crowd and feeling like we were there for the fun, food and festival just like everyone else.

We headed out the back doors to the food stalls,

buying a couple of mini cakes and a large cup of kombucha. Lily and Matt were sitting just inside the doorway and we grabbed a couple of seats next to them.

"Hey! Are you on next? Are you nervous?" Lily asked between bites of falafel.

"I am," I nodded and then pulled a face and giggled. "*Eeek!* I'm so glad you guys are here."

The sound technician came up and tapped me on the arm. "Okay, you're on in five. Ready?"

I braced myself, as I stood to follow him; my legs shaking; my heartbeat deafening in my ears.

You can do this, I told myself. *It's practice, that's all.*

Once upon a time, I'd been terrified of being on video camera too. Every time I tried to film something for our programs, I felt insanely nervous and completely stressed out. I knew I'd be better able to connect with and support my clients if I overcame this fear. So I kept going.

Shaking in my boots, but determined, I signed up to a group challenge and practiced every single day. Thirty days and thirty videos later, I could actually record a few minutes of footage without shaking all over the place like a nervous chihuahua. Consistency and repetition were key, as true in sobriety as it was in public speaking. Everything feels scary at first.

I realised the technician was saying something and I tried to focus. "I've put an extra microphone down the front there," he said, pointing to a mic stand in front of the stage. "So people can ask questions afterwards. Are you okay with doing a Q and A?"

I nodded numbly. I didn't have the courage to admit I wasn't prepared for that. Then I remembered that no one had asked any questions after the previous talk, so I needn't worry.

"Okay, you're on," he said, gesturing towards the podium. "Go for it."

~

The house lights dimmed as I took two wobbly steps towards the podium. I leaned into the microphone, my mind racing with all the public speaking tips I'd read in the days and weeks leading up to this moment.

Imagine the audience naked. Oh God, no, that wasn't going to help.

Find friendly faces and focus on those. Excellent, yes, that I could do. As I moved onto the second slide of my presentation, I scanned the room and was relieved to see Dom, Lily and Matt sitting in the middle row. Surprisingly, it looked as if more of the seats were filling up fast, and barely anyone was eating or drinking.

Not only that, but as I moved onto my third slide, I thought I could spot a few more faces smiling back at me. More and more people seemed to actually be listening and nodding along to what I was saying.

The blood continued to thunder through my brain. Almost all of the seats were now filled, while more people wandered in from outside and the other room to stand at the back and listen. After so diligently mentally preparing myself for the opposite, I was a little thrown by this, but in a good way.

I looked back at Dom and he grinned at me, wide-eyed, raising his eyebrows as if to say, *Check this out!*

As I reached my last slide and thanked everyone for listening, hot tears pricked my eyelids. In a split-second, not wanting to jinx it all, I decided to ignore the Q&A session suggestion altogether and instead dove off the side of the stage. I glanced at the sound technician. He looked back at me in surprise and then kind of shrugged and began setting up the stage for the next speaker.

When I was sure the coast was clear, I made my way over to find my friends. People were still shuffling their way into the other room, or outside, as I reached Dom.

"Well done!" he laughed, embracing me in a bear hug.

"Excuse me? Rebecca?" a voice said. I turned to see a blonde woman about my age. "That was such a great talk, thank you."

"Oh wow," I said, a little stunned. "Thank *you.*"

"I really liked the part where you talked about your drinking. I wondered if you had shared anything else about that online?"

"I have," I nodded, noticing the notepad she was holding. "Do you have a pen?"

As she pulled a pen from her handbag, I really wished I had some water, or a mint, or *something*. My mouth had turned into a desert and I was sure I had bad breath. I quickly wrote down my website addresses.

"Thank you so much," she smiled, leaning in to give me a hug.

"You're so welcome. It was lovely to meet you!" I hugged her back, trying not to breathe on her. I was overjoyed that she'd had the courage to come up and say hi, and felt rather silly that I'd chickened out on the Q&A session.

I turned to look for Dom again and noticed a small group of people standing close by, all looking at me. They smiled as I met their eyes, and it dawned on me that they were waiting to speak to me. I couldn't believe it.

Spotting Dom, I tried to catch his eye so I could signal that I needed my bag, and more importantly, the water and mints inside it, but he was engrossed in a conversation with Lily and Matt.

"Thank you so much for a wonderful talk, Rebecca," the man closest to me was saying. I turned to give him my full attention, praying I wouldn't scare him off with my dragon breath. He looked to be in his sixties or so, with kind eyes, and wearing a tweed beret that suited him perfectly. "The part where you talked about ways to drink more water really helped me because it's something I've always struggled with. I wondered if you could tell me more about that?" I grinned, thrilled at the chance for deeper connection, peppermints or not.

Fifteen minutes or so later, as the last person hugged me goodbye, I saw Dom approach.

"Wasn't that amazing?" I beamed at him. "People were listening; they actually came over to ask questions. And everyone was so lovely!"

"*You're* amazing," Dom laughed, pulling me in for another hug. "Come on, Lily wants to talk to you too."

As we reached their seats, Lily smiled and jumped up to hug me. "That was professional level, Bex! Honestly, most of the time when you watch a presentation it's like a game of 'count the *ummms*', but you didn't say *Um* once! That's unheard of."

"Really?" I giggled. The whole thing had passed in such a blur, I wasn't entirely sure *what* I'd said. "Thank you so much! Seeing your friendly faces looking back at me really helped."

"What do you want to do now?" Dom said. "These guys are planning to get some more food. You hungry?"

If there was one thing I wasn't feeling, it was hungry. Elated, yes. My brain short-circuiting as it attempted to process all of this, absolutely. And after all that adrenalin, quite possibly heading for a roller coaster of a crash.

"Or do you just want to head off?" Dom said, reading my mind.

I nodded gratefully and we hugged Lily and Matt

goodbye.

"I'll be honest," Dom said as we boarded the city-link bus, after I'd taken a huge swig from my water bottle and finally popped a peppermint into my mouth. "That was like a TED Talk!"

I laughed, thinking he was joking.

"I'm not blowing smoke up your butt," he said, catching my expression. "I'm serious." One look at him and I knew he was. If there was one thing Dom was, it was brutally honest. He wasn't afraid to tell me the truth, even when I sucked.

"See?" he said, waving his hands around animatedly. "You just need to believe in yourself. Can't you see yourself doing talks all over the world now? Maybe even a book tour or something?"

I laughed. It was so unlike him to get carried away - it was usually *me* with the overactive imagination - but I loved feeling his excitement.

Floating on Cloud Nine the whole way home, the high I felt after conquering this fear was infinitely better than any artificial high I'd ever experienced after a few glasses of wine. That feeling of surprising myself and feeling proud of myself was still so new, so unexpected, and so very spectacular.

FOUR

The dial tone purred down the line as I clicked the dashboard button on my computer and waited for it to connect. The best thing about these live class calls was that I could dial in while wearing fluffy tracksuit pants. Class began at 9:00am and I was right on time, armed with a cup of hot coffee, a notebook and pen.

Always one for perfect attendance, I'd dialled in to the two prior calls. This was the last scheduled call before the holiday break and I was excited to give it my full attention. I was preoccupied with preparing for the speaking event before, but now that the event was delightfully out of the way, I was all ears.

Music began to play down the line, before a warm,

American, female voice said, "Welcome everyone!"

The instructor started her presentation, sharing several tips for book writing organisation, while I sipped my coffee and scribbled down notes.

Suddenly I froze as something she'd just said hit me. The words were still reordering themselves in my head and I held my breath, hoping she'd say them again. As if by magic, she did. "Books are forever."

I stared into space as the magnitude of that one little sentence echoed around my skull. I thought of all my clients, and all the other women out there who might be struggling with exactly what I went through, and all the beautiful souls who'd ever written to tell me that my words had helped them to feel less alone. *Books are forever.*

An idea was forming and I could almost *feel* it taking shape, rearranging things inside my head, sticking a sharp heel right into denial's backside. *What if,* instead of trying to do a million different things in order to help more people - instead of desperately cramming more and more things into my boat while it slowly sank - I wrote a book? *One project* that, once completed, could live on, helping more people and having a greater impact in the world? *Books are forever.*

I glanced up at my wall calendar. Dom and I were about to wind down for the holidays. All of our gifts were under our very sparkly tree, and we were looking forward to spending time with friends and family.

Unless! I thought to myself, impulsively ripping my calendar right off the wall as inspiration struck.

I had no client sessions scheduled for the next three weeks and the construction crew always closed down over the holidays. *What if I worked straight through? Could I catch up with the class by then? Was it even possible? Did I dare even try?*

My gaze fell to Amy's book, still sitting proudly on my shelf. Years earlier, out at a bar one Friday night with colleagues, a woman from another team that I didn't know very well said, "If you could do, or be, anything in the world, what would it be?" She'd directed the question at our group in general, before pointing to me. "Rebecca, you start."

"An Author," I blurted, emboldened by the booze, before I could stop myself from sharing my most precious and personal dream with the very same people I'd see in broad daylight come Monday morning. The minute the words left my lips, a deep blush enveloped my cheeks, despite the vast number of vodkas I'd drunk.

"So go and do that!" she said, throwing her hands up in exasperation, splashing the drink out of her glass in the process. "What are you waiting for? Stop wasting time! Go and do that!"

The rest of us had looked at each other and laughed at her intensity, but afterwards, I couldn't get that conversation out of my mind. The truth was, I talked about a lot of things I intended to do when I was drinking. Big, bold plans written on the backs of napkins, shared with friends over our tenth round, and drunkenly scrawled into my journal late at night.

Plans that magically evaporated like stardust in the morning light.

These were the kinds of milestones I only ever talked about; never taking inspired action, and hating myself for it. There was always something for me to hide behind. Whether it was a crushing hangover or my latest drama, there was always something to distract me and keep me from doing the deeper work.

I told myself I was impossibly busy. So busy that I couldn't possibly fit another thing into my already overflowing schedule. These were good reasons for not getting tangled up in a new project right now; solid reasons.

Not the real reasons, though. Deep down, in some part of me I never liked to look into, I knew why. I was scared. Scared of trying and failing at the one dream I'd had in my heart since I was a little girl. Before I could read; before I could even tell you how or why the dream was imprinted on my heart, it was there.

If I tried now and it didn't work, what then? How does a person carry on when their biggest, boldest lifelong dream is shattered?

And yet... Wasn't this exactly why I'd embraced sobriety in the first place; to tackle the wondrous, scary dreams and find out what I was truly made of? It didn't matter if my biggest, boldest dream had always been to become a published author, or direct a theatre group, or run a marathon. If I wasn't going to actually try for the big one, I was only kidding myself that I was trying at all.

And really, was there really *ever* a convenient time to turn your life upside down, whether we were talking about conducting a sobriety experiment, starting a family, or adopting a puppy? Didn't everyone simply start before they were ready?

That funny look Ben had given me played over in my head while a fire began to burn in my belly.

~

Jenna and I met the following week at one of our favourite cafes in the city. I made sure to arrive early, well before her scheduled lunch break, but try as I might, I still couldn't secure us a table in the courtyard sunshine. The bustling holiday crowds meant there was only one small table remaining just inside the cafe. I plonked myself down gratefully, happy that there was a table left at all.

Excited chatter echoed around the cafe walls, and I enjoyed soaking up the fun, festive atmosphere. Sunlight sparkled from the rows of tinsel hanging across the courtyard. The weather was warming up and the busy city crowd wore sharp suits and flouncy dresses designed to take them from office to party.

A well-dressed man wearing a Santa hat and a cheeky grin rushed by, carrying a box wrapped in reindeer gift paper. I watched as a large group outside laughed and cheered as he approached.

Just then I spotted Jenna hurrying through the

door.

"Hi honey!" I squealed and waved, jumping up to hug her hello. Jenna had been one of my favourite people in the team I last worked for. We'd bonded instantly and had chuckled our way through almost daily coffee breaks. Now, more than two years since we'd last worked together, we still met up every month or so over lunch. Jenna had been witness to every step of my kooky entrepreneurial journey.

"I can't believe it's almost Christmas!" she said, draping her handbag across the back of her chair as she sat down. "What are you up to for the holidays, chickie? Got much planned?"

"Well!" I said, before pausing dramatically, wanting to make sure she was listening. I was so excited by this crazy new idea and could only hope my excitement was contagious.

"I've batched a heap of work, and cleared my calendar of any appointments for the next three weeks, and… I'm planning a little writing retreat. I'm going to write a book!"

Jenna blinked at me. "As in, write the whole thing?" she balked. "In three weeks?"

"Yep!" I chirped, thoroughly enchanted with the idea. Images of oak bookshelves, first edition hardbacks, and beautiful vintage typewriters swam before my eyes. *Oh, the glorious romance of it all!*

I was so pumped by the relative and unexpected success of my talk, I felt like anything was possible. Plus I quite liked the idea of having a passion project to devote myself to throughout the silly season. There'd be no fears of missing out on the usual festive folly for me, oh no, I'd be incredibly busy being a Real Writer. Minus the stereotypical drink in hand, obviously.

"Is that not really fast?" Jenna giggled, rousing me from my fantasy.

"Well, my book class made it sound simple enough. Write your outline. Fill in the outline. Done!" I met her eyes and we both dissolved into laughter.

"It'll take a bit of hard work, of course," I conceded, wiping away tears of amusement. "But seriously, I think I can do it. I *have* to. The construction crew are on their holiday break for three weeks. It's the only time I'll have peace and quiet during the day."

"Okay," Jenna nodded, suddenly all matter-of-fact as though we were still working together in Project Management. "When's your class deadline?"

"We're aiming for a publication date of May first. I'll need to catch up to my class, of course, but that's…" I counted them out on my fingers. "One, two, three, four months from now." *Four months?* That didn't sound right. Surely I had longer than that?

Jenna dissolved back into giggles. "To finish the whole thing and publish it? Don't books usually take many, many months to write, chickie? Or *years,* even?"

"I guess," I swallowed as the thought sank its way into my stomach. "But I can always publish it later…" I nodded, more for my reassurance than hers. "If I don't make the class deadline."

"Well then, I think it's a brilliant plan!" she declared, lifting her menu and becoming engrossed in the choices in front of her.

And it *was* a brilliant plan. Okay, so perhaps a rather ambitious one, but a writing retreat would make all the difference in the world. I was almost perfectly certain of it.

FIVE

I had every intention of sticking to my writing retreat. Unfortunately, my body had other plans. After a hectic year, it made it very clear - in no uncertain terms - that it just needed to rest, striking me down with the worst head cold I'd had in years.

"You're not Superwoman," Dom said as I battled against it, trying and failing to somehow will it out of my system. "I know you like to think you are."

"But I don't *get* sick!" I protested. I was flabbergasted as to why, when I only experienced a cold every few years or so, it had to happen right this minute. Why *now*, when I had *Seriously Big Plans?*

"Everyone gets sick," Dom shrugged, passing me

the tissues.

I knew I could shake myself out of it, though, I was sure of it. I didn't have *time* to be sick. I didn't want to spend days under a blanket; I wanted to write a *book*, dammit!

"What do you always say to me when I get sick?" Dom said, interrupting my pity party.

"Don't fight it," I sniffed. "Find a way to make it fun."

Dom nodded. "There you go."

It was true. Whenever he was unwell, I reminded him that battling against what was only made it worse. I always encouraged him to get comfy on the couch with a big cosy quilt and his favourite television show, and drink endless cups of tea.

I figured it was like emotions; fighting against them only made it worse. Surrendering to them made them pass along much more quickly. As one of my friends once said, "like clouds across a sky."

"Fine," I sighed, collapsing into the couch.

The holiday season passed in a flash. By the time my first class of the new year rolled around, I'd recovered from the cold but was still no closer to having any words on the page.

Utterly flustered that I was falling even further behind, I tried writing again, but the construction crew were back. Their jackhammering, grinding and drilling had been going on for three entire years now and these guys hadn't even finished the *foundations* yet. We'd never seen anything like it. Whenever we bumped into our neighbours, it was all any of us could ever talk about.

"Can you believe these guys? How long before they reach the surface? Why are there only six guys building this entire thing?"

Our noise-cancelling headphones could only do so much. This was the kind of noise I could feel reverberating through my rib cage.

"*Arrrgggg!* We need to *move!*" I wailed to Dom. "I'm serious. I can't take it anymore!" I was so tearful lately; so tired from my workload and the ridiculous noise that made it impossible to get on top of my 'To Do' list. Moving was the answer, I was sure of it. Moving would fix everything.

Three years earlier, when Dom and I had searched for our current apartment - our first rental home together - in the midst of a crazy property price boom that had sent demand and prices sky-high, every inspection was packed to the brim with other people also trying to secure a rental. We'd looked at some scary apartments back then, many located right next to the freeway, or with creepy parking lots, or zero privacy. And yet, after we'd spent the better part of a month asking for time off work to chase home-open appointments all over town, I was impatient to just pick one already!

But Dom wouldn't be rushed into it. "It has to feel right," he repeated after we'd viewed apartments nine, ten, eleven and twelve.

By week five and apartment number fourteen, I

was beginning to lose hope of ever finding one we were both happy with. Apartment fourteen wasn't in any of the neighbourhoods we'd originally had our hearts set on. In the online photos, it looked dated and a little run down. I almost suggested we skip the viewing altogether, but in the interest of playing the numbers game, we went along.

As I walked into the apartment, my heart sank. Dom, being a designer, had a keen eye for aesthetics, and when I saw the decades-old floor tiles and decor, I thought for sure this one would bomb as well.

Instead, he walked into the middle of the apartment, paused for a second, and then with a big smile, announced, "I like it!"

"But… the tiles…?" I stuttered in bewilderment. "The area…? It's not what we were looking for…?"

"It feels right," he said. And that was that.

Back then we had no idea we'd soon be working from home and would thrive in an area buzzing with the energy of entrepreneurs and start-up companies, rather than in the suburbs. We had no idea we'd love our local cafes, or that our neighbours would be so kind and lovely.

We also had no idea that a construction crew was about to move in next door, of course, but that was another beast altogether. Back then, my fear of missing out overruled my judgement and would have had us living in a matchbox on the freeway if it weren't for Dom's intuition, patience and common sense.

The apartment hadn't evolved with us, though.

Just like in sobriety, just because something was good for you in the beginning didn't mean it would work for you three years on, whether we were talking about friendships, work or hobbies. As much as I loved to cling to the old, I was starting to learn when to let go and move forward.

We'd been talking about moving house for weeks. Our lease was almost up for renewal, and as much as we'd loved the apartment itself, this was a chance to make our escape.

"There's one available on our favourite street," I'd told Dom, knowing full well what he'd say.

"Too small," he said, confirming my predictions. "But if it's still available after the holidays, I guess it couldn't hurt to go see it."

Well, *this* was a turn of events! "Really? But I thought you said..."

"Let's just go *see*," he said.

And now, here we were. The first week of the new year, and by some miracle the online ad said it was still available. My heart took that as a big, honkin' green light, of course. The hunt was on.

~

While we loved all of our neighbourhood, there was one street in particular that we loved the most. As a side street, it was spared from thoroughfare traffic. Lined with mature, leafy trees, it was also two streets closer to the city and to the botanical gardens we loved to walk in. It was short and sweet and perfect.

With the city still waking up after the holiday break, and no official home opens scheduled, Dom called the agent and made an appointment for a private viewing. We met in front of the building at 2:00pm.

"Hi guys," the agent called as she crossed the street towards us. She was carrying a brown, leather folio and a bundle of electronic fobs and keys that *jingle-jangled* as she walked. "Come on up."

Her heels obediently added to the symphony, *click-clacking* across the gleaming lobby as we followed her inside. Dom and I exchanged glances as she pressed the button into the elevator for the seventh floor. *So far, so good.*

The lift opened onto a small landing with just four doors.

"Umm, it's this one," the agent nodded, leading us to one of the doors and flicking through her keys, attempting to find the right one. With a click, the door opened into a dim, narrow corridor that led all the way through to the balcony and the view beyond.

"As you can see, it's all brand new," she said as Dom and I gravitated towards the blue skies at the end of the corridor. The living room had a tiny, galley kitchen and barely enough room for a couple of couches, but all of that was a far-distant concern after witnessing the massive wall of glass that framed the large balcony. Dom pulled open the double-height sliding door and we stepped out into the warm summer air. Spread before us was a magnificent view. The city's skyscrapers twinkled in the afternoon sunlight. To our left we could see for miles, and to the right, treetops in the nearby botanical gardens.

I couldn't believe this place was in our price range. Thrilled, I turned to look at Dom but I couldn't read his expression.

We headed in to look at the rest of the apartment, which consisted of just two small bedrooms and bathrooms. There was zero storage space.

I lingered in the second bedroom that could potentially become my home office. Someday we dreamt of having a three bedroom place, but for now, Dom was happy to work from the living room while I needed a door I could close for my video calls.

The room had a small window that overlooked the neighbouring apartment building. Regardless of the lack of view, all I could think about was the sweet, enveloping silence in that room.

My mind went into overdrive, calculating our options. We could potentially afford a larger place further from the city, and we'd talked about it, but honestly, I viewed that option as the kiss of death for us. There was every danger that we'd sink into the comfort of regular life and lose all motivation to be creative entrepreneurs. Whether completely unfounded or not, I worried I'd lose sight of my precious, newly discovered passion, and without that, I didn't see how I'd ever have the strength to stay sober. I'd finally found something that I loved to do. I *needed* this, and I had to make sure I fiercely protected it.

Thanking the agent, Dom and I headed back down in the lift, and out into the nearby alley that served as a shortcut to our apartment. I could barely contain myself until we were completely out of earshot.

"*Soooo?* What did you think?" I asked Dom, trying to stop myself from skipping alongside him. I wanted his honest opinion before I produced mine, just in case my skewed judgement had gotten it wrong. Although it was something I was actively working on in sobriety, I wasn't sure I was entirely back in touch with my intuition. I still didn't trust myself not to be swayed by a pretty, modern interior, or to be driven by my fear of missing out.

"I love it," Dom said. "Those high ceilings remind me of a New York loft style apartment, or an art gallery."

"I know!" I gushed, still picturing myself in that silent room. "And it's all so new and pretty. And that view is amazing." I paused as my doubts shoved a boot in the door. "But is it too small? I mean, it's definitely Manhattan or Tokyo sized. But I'm sure people in those places work from home all the time too, right? We could watch all those 'Tiny House' shows and embrace it as a big adventure?"

"We'll make it work," Dom assured me.

But back in our apartment, those niggling doubts were making a big cosy bed for themselves in my head. "We'd have to sell or donate at least half of our furniture," I prattled on, looking around our current living room. "There's no room for this big dining table, for example. Or our coffee table, or those cupboards in my office. Which means we'd also have to clear out everything stored inside them…"

"Okay," Dom nodded, as though it were no big deal.

"But… will people think we're bonkers, moving into such a small space when we both work from home?"

"What people?" he said.

"Well…" I huffed, waving my arms about in a gesture intended to include everyone we'd ever invite over; living or imaginary. "Friends? Family?"

"Nah," he grinned, knowing full well that they would.

"Are you sure?" I pushed, unnerved by how much I wanted this. "I mean, aren't we already weird enough?" I said as I counted them off on my fingers. "Vegan. Sober. Creative entrepreneurs… and now modern minimalists by force of a tiny apartment. Nothing about us is normal."

"So?" He shrugged. "Who wants to be normal?"

He had a point.

On New Years Eve, I'd declared this to be the year of 'less, but better', a devotion to quality over quantity in every area of my life. One of my clients had once called this "consciously curating our lives" and I just loved that.

Now here it was; a challenge to really walk the

talk. We could part with half of our worldly possessions and I could wake up every morning to blue skies for miles and sweet, sweet serenity in which to write a book. Or I could sink back into my cosy comfort zone.

That night I tossed and turned, unable to sleep. My mind was stuck in a hamster wheel; imagining myself in that room writing in complete and heavenly silence, followed by claustrophobically climbing the walls after working in such a small apartment together all day. Alert with nervous and excited energy, I was convinced this would either be the very best or the very worst move we'd ever made; for us, and for our fledgling venture.

There was every chance that our application would be rejected, of course. Everyone knew that landlords were typically not big fans of the self-employed.

My heart and my fear continued to battle it out. I didn't know which outcome to root for.

~

Tired but wired, I felt exceptionally emotional as the jackhammering started up again the following morning. It was only during our mid-morning walk to escape the noise that Dom's phone finally rang. We both stopped dead in the street as he produced the phone from his pocket. Inhaling sharply, we looked at the screen. It was the real estate agent.

"Quick! Answer it!" I squealed.

"Hello, Dominic speaking," he said, ever the calmest ship in the storm, never giving anything away. I turned to look up at the nearby trees in an attempt to quell my nerves. It was no use. I looked back towards Dom.

"Yes," he said into the phone, nodding. I instructed every bone in my body to be patient, while all I really wanted to do was tug on his arm and wail, "Yes *whaaaaat?* Did we get it? Did we?"

Dom saw my puppy dog eyes and held up a finger as if to say, 'wait.'

The phone call lasted approximately a year and a half. Finally, he hung up the phone.

"Well?" I said.

"Sooooo…" He paused, taking a deep breath, knowing full well that the suspense would kill me, and enjoying every second of it.

"Tell *meeee!*" I wailed, shaking him by the shoulders until he started laughing.

"We got it!" He picked me up and spun me around.

"*Squeeeee!*" I laughed, as he set me back down. "Oh my goodness, this is it! No more headphones. No more headaches, or having to do all our creative work on weekends. No more having to schedule recordings around their construction racket."

"And a quiet place for you to write the book."

"Uh-huh." I nodded. Naturally, I'd meant that too. "So when do we get the keys?"

Dom smiled. "About four weeks from now."

"Okay, so we're going to have to start selling stuff and getting ready," I rambled. "This is so exciting!"

List geek that I was, I couldn't wait to get back to my office and locate a pen and paper. This move would cause quite a big delay to my planned timeline for the book, of course, but I was sure I'd have time to at least create the outline before moving day. Then I could get straight onto writing in the new room.

Really, there's no point trying to write in our current place anyway, I nodded to myself as a mental handshake to my new plan. *The first draft deserves more respect than to be written in the midst of all this noise. Better to wait until I have my new, pretty, quiet office.*

That night, Dom and I celebrated with sparkling kombucha in crystal flutes. From our living room window, we could just see a glimpse of our new building. The golden sunset danced across its shiny surfaces, as though symbolising the start of something greater.

"To our new home," Dom said, raising his glass.

"Cheers," I beamed, clinking my glass against his.

Dom pulled me in for a hug. "I was telling Anthony earlier. He wondered if we'd been suffering from Stockholm Syndrome."

I giggled. Our friends and family had often joked about our predicament, especially when we'd often tell them we couldn't go see them on Sundays because it was the only day we could enjoy our home in silence.

I gazed at the new building. I'd quit drinking in our current apartment. The new one would be the first home I'd ever live in completely sober as an adult. A new home offered a fresh slate; a new beginning. And potentially a place where my lifelong writing dream would come true. Or was forever shattered apart.

SIX

As our moving date inched ever closer, I began to experience a range of mystifying flashbacks. One annoyingly persistent memory was of something that had happened almost a decade earlier. My ex and I had moved into our new house and were delighted to meet our new neighbours. A softly spoken minister and his beautiful family, they grew their own veggies and played musical instruments together. One of his daughters even built her own violin from scratch.

One day they kindly invited us over for dinner. It was a Friday and we knew they didn't drink. Not able to even comprehend the thought of going alcohol-free on a Friday night, we hatched what we thought was a brilliant plan. We'd simply drink before we went; enough to keep us happily satisfied all through dinner.

Only, that 'just right' level was so hard to get right. Misjudging, I drank too much, and the next day, could barely even remember the second half of dinner.

At the time, I was so steeped in shame and regret that I'd hidden from our neighbours for months, sprinting from the garage into the house, desperate to avoid bumping into them as they checked their mail or took their bins out.

Now that I was sober and finally had the emotional maturity to comprehend just how childish that behaviour had been, all that shame and regret was only amplified.

You're not that person anymore, I reminded myself. *Forgive yourself.*

Clearly it was the move that was triggering all this, and I had to believe the flashbacks were driven by a deep fear of not being good enough; of not feeling worthy or deserving of being there, in a beautiful home and my favourite neighbourhood.

The logical part of my brain knew I'd made mistakes but that I'd changed, and deserved health and happiness. And yet, it seemed the memo sometimes wasn't getting through to the deepest, darkest parts of me.

There was only one thing for it. If it was too noisy to start writing in our current apartment, the least I could do was hurry the move along.

"Let's declutter some more!" I hollered out to Dom from my office.

I'd always known this room would be hard. Not only was it my office, but because it was our only spare room, the wardrobe and cabinets were stuffed with photo albums, old diaries, souvenirs, clothes we wore once in a blue moon, and random sporting equipment.

As a woman who'd struggled with sentimentality in the past, I was determined not to let nostalgia slow me down. I knew I'd come across long-lost important papers and forgotten treasures and I was determined to march on regardless.

I'd already decluttered so much when I'd first embarked on my sobriety experiment. But, as they say, you never know quite how much stuff you have until you move.

Dom popped his head around the doorframe. "Remember to get those skates out," he instructed before disappearing again.

We'd already taken several car loads of donations to a local charity shop, and Dom had started selling some of our furniture on second-hand sites, as well as bravely parting with his beloved bike and electric guitar.

With our fledgling enterprise in its infancy and not ready for us to take a salary, we were still living extremely modestly on what was left of our life savings. Despite the lack of space at the new apartment, being forced to sell things we no longer needed was actually quite helpful as far as helping to keep us afloat.

I opened the wardrobe and moved a few boxes until I could reach my beloved roller-skates. I'd ordered them online during a random retro phase, but I hadn't skated in quite a few years.

I picked up the left boot. The skates were practically new, all shiny black with pink and green fluorescent stripes. One of the sparkly pink wheels spun around, mesmerising me.

What if I get into it again?, I thought to myself. I mean, I need fun, sober stuff to do now, right? Surely I'll go again? With a swift nod, I placed them on the 'still deciding' pile on the floor.

Looking around the room, I was overwhelmed with the prospect of what to tackle next. In my previous job in the city, I'd spent most of my lunch breaks shopping. All these clothes and accessories had seemed so vitally important at the time. It was only on the day I resigned that I realised freedom felt so much better than shopping ever did, and that all this stuff had been a way of distracting myself from the fact that I wasn't doing work I cared about.

Little did I know, of course, that I was about to work for my most critical and demanding boss yet: myself.

Biting my lip, I figured a change of direction might help. "I'll start on the filing cabinet," I called out, more to give myself permission than to notify Dom.

My jewellery box sat on the top of the filing cabinet and as I moved it, a shiny little object peeked out from underneath. It was a silver bracelet I'd completely forgotten about. I wore it constantly in early sobriety. Engraved inside, on the part that no one else could see but that I knew was there, were the words: 'Stay here'.

As I turned it over in my hands, a surge of memories flooded my senses. Those first few weeks of sobriety had been so hard. I was terrified of a life without alcohol. I honestly believed I'd never have - or *be* - fun, ever again.

I attended a heap of events in those first few weeks, and I wore the bracelet to every single one. It acted as a symbol, helping to remind me *why* I was doing this hard thing: to experience a deeper, more honest relationship with Dom, to pour my heart and soul into my creative endeavours, and to experience more freedom and joy in life. It silently encouraged me to 'stay here', on the scary but oh-so-rewarding sober side.

The truth was, I was a different person when I moved into this apartment three years earlier; still drinking, still believing I needed alcohol to be happy. I had bigger, bolder dreams now. More importantly, I had evidence that I could create and achieve things that I previously believed impossible, if I only applied myself.

I knew what I had to do. Moving my skates to the 'selling' pile, I picked up a nearby box I'd previously packed and emptied its contents onto the floor. Time was ticking. The removalists were booked. It couldn't all come with us. It was time to let go.

~

"Okay, that's everything," the Removalist said. "Sign here."

Dom scribbled his signature on the form and the Removalist trundled out the door with his trolley.

"Thank you," I called, closing the door behind him.

"Finally," Dom said. It was a marathon move spanning more than six hours. The guys turned up with a truck half the size we were expecting while the weather was twice as hot.

I checked my phone. It was still thirty-nine degrees celsius outside, which may as well have been a hundred.

"Well at least it wasn't rain or hail," I half-joked to Dom.

"Let's crank the air con. Where's the remote?"

"I put it in my bag somewhere… here it is!" I said, pulling it out triumphantly.

Dom followed me down the corridor. I couldn't wait to collapse on the couch for a minute to catch my breath and recover.

It was only then that we sensed something might be a little off. Naturally, there were boxes stacked everywhere that would eventually be put away. But as we attempted to shuffle our way into the living room, we realised we couldn't get to the couches, or to the balcony door. We couldn't move at all. The room was jam packed with furniture. It was like a giant Jenga game. My brain couldn't comprehend how we were going to make sense of it all.

"Well…" I trailed off, trying to think of a logical first step. "They say you should set up your bedroom first, so you have somewhere to crash when you're too exhausted to unpack any more," I suggested. "Shall we look for the sheets?"

Dom looked defeated but nodded. "Let's do that."

As we made the bed, my mind was still ticking over; still trying to make sense of the riddle in the living room. We'd sold our dining table with the intention of someday buying a smaller one but I couldn't see how even a tiny one might fit.

"Do you think maybe we'll have to find smaller dining chairs eventually?" I pondered.

"I think we're going to have to forgo having a dining *anything*," Dom said.

"Oh," I said quietly, too exhausted to fight the idea. "But… where will we eat?"

"We can have TV dinners," he suggested. "Balance our meals on our laps."

I giggled at that image, thinking back to all the tiny house shows we'd watched over the past few weeks. "What about that episode where they just brought out a folding table whenever they wanted to have friends over?"

"That could work," Dom said, pulling a pillow out of a nearby box. "We might be able to store it in the carpark, and bring it up when we need it. We could use our desk chairs as multi-purpose dining chairs."

"We might have to sell some more furniture from my office too," I said, thinking out loud.

Dom nodded. "We have to face the fact that we're in a tiny space now. Regular house furniture won't work."

I nodded, relieved to have at least some semblance of a plan. This would all mean a disruption to my schedule to start writing in my new office, of course. I'd need to help Dom sell it all, and then to give away more of our belongings, now that we'd have no furniture for storage.

But that was fine. We were away from the noise, and that's all that mattered. I could easily catch up with the writing once we'd sorted out our space. I'd fly along the page once the move was completely finished and peace and order was restored to our galaxy, I was sure of it.

~

I was thrilled that Lily was to be my first official visitor. Being a Friday, she'd decided to take a longer lunch break and we agreed it'd be hilarious fun to see if we could spot her office from our new balcony.

I pranced around the apartment while I waited for

her. I'd made a bunch of fancy salads that were now chilling in the fridge, along with a jug of the latest fruity mocktail recipe I'd been experimenting with.

Dom and I still hadn't gotten around to buying a folding table yet, so I figured we could sit on the office chairs on the balcony and pretend it was a picnic. By this point, I was just glad we'd sold some furniture so she could move at all in the apartment.

I jumped as the intercom buzzed. It felt like we'd done nothing but unpack and work like mad for the past two weeks. I was so excited to see a friendly face.

"Hi!" I squealed at the front door, as we hugged hello.

"Oh wow, the view!" Lily said, spotting it from the front door.

"Right?" I grinned, pulling her inside. "That was what clinched it. We figured the view would keep us from getting cabin fever."

Lily followed me into the living room and we stood staring out at it for a few moments. Sunlight glittered off the city buildings, and a flock of birds flew by. Unlike the intense heat of our moving day, this was the perfect summer's day. It was the kind of day where you couldn't help but feel joyful and relaxed, with an all-enveloping warmth that felt like a huge hug.

"Come on, let me show you the rest."

The first door off the living room was my new office. I giggled as I posed in the middle of the room. "It's tiny, I know, but *listen*. Hear that? No noise!"

She chuckled and pointed to my desk that I'd positioned facing the window. "So this is where you're writing?"

"Mmhhmm," I nodded, although I knew full well that I hadn't yet written a word. It wasn't that I didn't want to, of course, it was just that I was so crazy busy. There was unpacking still to do; and coaching; an upcoming mastermind to organise; a yoga class I'd signed up for at my local studio; organising a house-warming party; and a million other things. This move had always been about creating balance as well as escaping the noise. I'd catch up on writing once this stuff was out of the way. *Easy peasy*, I assured myself. Plus, all the newsletters and social posts I wrote each week counted, surely. I was writing *something*.

Sure you are, a little voice piped up inside me. A scratchy feeling crawled its way across my chest. Annoyingly it felt very similar to the sensation I used to experience when I made excuses for my drinking.

"Come on, let's go have some lunch," I said, leading Lily out of my office as fast as possible.

We were expecting many family visits over the weekend and despite having been excited earlier to show them my new office, I suddenly felt a sinking dread, imagining them all asking that very same question. *So this is where you're writing?*

SEVEN

By the time Tuesday morning rolled around, I was sick to death of the gnawing feeling inside. It'd been weeks since I'd dialled into my first class call from my new office. Weeks since my heart sank as our lecturer advised, "By now you should have finalised the content of your manuscript." While I'd successfully created the outline, I hadn't even *started* on the actual manuscript.

My next class call was just a week away. Determined not to fall further behind, I'd powered like a maniac through my usual workload all week. Now I'd have an entire day to focus on writing. I was ready to *Make Things Happen.*

My computer display read 8:32am as I opened a blank document.

My sister once said, "I don't want to read books that just tell me what to do. I want to read someone else's story and learn from what *they* did." When I stopped to think about that, it made perfect sense. In witnessing other people's stories, we recognised our own, and understood that we weren't alone.

The thought of sharing my own story still made me feel queasy, but I recognised that as a sign that it was exactly what I needed to do.

I took a deep breath and typed: 'How it all began.'

This is it!, I cheered inside my own head, throwing virtual pom-poms into the air. *This is the intro to my book. I'm doing it. I'm writing!*

I hit 'return' and paused. Stuck on the next sentence, I sat motionless like a sleeping lizard. Staring at the screen, a dizzying number of flashbacks swam before my eyes, turning my stomach. Every cell in my body screamed, 'Run!'

It's just the beginning that feels like opening Pandora's Box, I assured myself, using stubborn, brute force to stay put. *It will get easier from here.*

I fumbled as I typed, attempting to capture some of the stories my subconscious had decided to unlock, while the depth of emotion shocked and overwhelmed me.

I needed a calming cup of tea. I mean, real writers drank tea, didn't they? I was sure I'd read that somewhere. Surely tea will help.

Hightailing it to the kitchen, I lunged at the kettle, my fingers still trembling as I filled it with water. Dom was typing away at his workstation in the corner, completely oblivious to my impending nervous breakdown.

His desk overlooked the neighbouring apartment building. As I walked over to him, a familiar figure caught my eye in the distance.

"Oh!" I practically shouted, causing Dom to jump in fright. "There she is again!"

"What?" he said after he'd recovered from his heart attack. "Who?"

I pointed. "There! The woman in the apartment over there. I've seen her tapping away at her keyboard for days now. *Weeks,* even! I wonder if she's writing a book?"

Dom followed my line of sight, nodding as he spotted her. "Uh-huh. She might be. Does that inspire you to move your butt?"

"Maybe," I giggled.

"Well, hop to it, missy!" He wandered over to the kitchen counter and started making a pot of tea.

I stood watching the woman for a few moments, wondering what she was really working on. I tried conjuring a telepathic spell, demanding that her passion and dedication waft over to our apartment and envelop me.

I was just in the process of closing my eyes in order to double down on the spell when a voice nudged its way around my head like a puppy under a blanket. It was something a friend had said once: "Because how we do *one* thing is how we do *everything*."

My eyes flew open. *Oh my God.* Wasn't this exactly like what I'd done with my drinking? Believed if only I moved to a new city, or changed my career, then the problem would magically disappear? Now here I was, thinking that if I moved somewhere quieter, my procrastination would magically disappear.

Just as I'd discovered with sobriety, the only way the issue would ever be resolved was if I tried something different and modified my behaviour. The buck stopped here.

"Right, that's it!" I announced. "No more messing around. I'm a Serious Writer now!"

Storming the few steps back to my office, I noticed my desk looked a little messy; not like a serious writer's desk at all. I quickly tidied the pens and books on my desk, filing away a few papers.

Satisfied, I got comfy in my chair, ready to tackle this thing.

To my surprise, I managed to stay there. In fact, two hours passed in what felt like minutes. I was having a ball.

"Are you writing?" Dom said, peering around the doorframe, checking on me.

I smiled, delighted to show him my handiwork. "I am. I'm just making a plan of when to write. Like a study plan. I'm *preparing* to write, in other words, which as everybody knows, is just as important."

"Is it?"

"Yep! See?" I shuffled the papers around on my desk so I could show him the calendars and schedules I'd meticulously drawn up for the next few months, adorned with pretty ink and colourful stickers. "And this writing software is a total game changer. Holy moly, it's *so* much better than using just blank documents. I honestly don't even know how I got to this point without it. Someone in my class shared a discount code so I've downloaded it and I'm doing the tutorials. It's taking a while to get through it all but teaching myself this now will pay dividends when I start writing."

"Uh huh." Dom stared at me, completely unconvinced. "Don't you think you should actually get started on writing the book?"

"But... I have to know how and when I plan to write, don't I? If you fail to plan, you plan to fail." I'd heard that last line somewhere, and as a natural born planner, I adored the permission it gave me to go nuts with lists and schedules and budgets.

Dom sighed and sat in the spare chair. "So you know that audiobook I love to listen to?"

I tapped my pen against my teeth as I thought it over. "*Ummm...* The spaceship one?"

Dom nodded. "So there's this part where one of the guys has a big exam to study for, so he decides to draw up a meticulous study plan to ensure he makes enough time to prep. Only, he sleeps in the first day and misses his first scheduled session. So he decides to draw up a whole new plan, with new deadlines, to fit the amount of time he has left. Only, the next day he drinks too much caffeine or something, and has to be hospitalised. So he misses his next scheduled session, and decides he needs to draw up a whole new plan for the amount of time he has left. He keeps doing this until the day of the exam; forever making new study plans and never actually hitting the books." Dom paused to give me a meaningful look. "So," he said, leaning back in his chair. "Do you get what I'm saying?"

I attempted a sigh of resignation that came out as more of a groan. "Less planning; more action?"

Dom smiled as he stood to leave the room. "Exactly."

As he closed the door behind him, I knew he was right.

But really, it wouldn't make sense not to finish the calendars first.

~

After I created my shiny, pretty writing schedule, I dreamt up a delightful idea to create a collection of alcohol-free drink recipes as a little bonus to go with the book.

The extra workload would create more pressure, but I was convinced it'd be worth it. I mean, how delicious would it be to sip a mocktail while reading a book about sobriety? Besides, I figured I could easily squeeze this project in if I just got up a little earlier each day.

Dom had been called to an early meeting with one of his web design clients, which I saw as the perfect opportunity to experiment in the kitchen while he wasn't working from the opposite corner of the room.

Lining up various citrus fruits along the kitchen bench, I thought about a book I'd read years before. It suggested that humans succumbed to drama or addiction because they weren't actively creating something.

When I'd first read that, I felt like the wind had been knocked out of me. Fascinated, it had played on my mind ever since. As much as I'd once fallen for the somewhat tired stereotype of the drunken writer, alcohol had only served to suck the energy and creativity right out of me.

When I'd first started my recipe blog, I convinced myself that maybe *that* was my creative calling: to write funny little stories to go along with each recipe. But it wasn't long before I confirmed what I'd always suspected: I was effectively a one-woman hurricane in the kitchen; choc chips and soy sauce flying everywhere.

I'd just managed to create another drink concoction when I heard Dom coming through the front door. He entered the kitchen slowly, goggling at me. "What are you doing?"

"I'm being creative!" I informed him proudly.

His eyes fell to the pile of dishes in the sink, the abandoned blender filled with what was now a sick-ly-green liquid, and the squished pomegranate seeds that had rendered the chopping board a virtual crime scene. Sticky orange juice covered the entire kitchen bench, but I didn't have time to think about that.

"Here, taste this," I said, shoving a glass of amber liquid under his nose. "What do you think?"

Dom took a sip and then gave me *the look*. "Do you really have time to be mucking about with this? What time's your client session?"

"It's at ten," I said. "I'm almost ready. But I've gotta' come up with these recipes too. What do you think?"

"Tastes good," he nodded, handing the glass back to me before heading to my office to set up my computer for the call.

Hhmmm, I thought, taking a sip. Just good? Was that good enough to be included in the recipe collection?

I jotted down the ingredients, hoping I could tweak them later and create something that might elicit a more enthusiastic response.

Quickly checking that my shirt was free of stains, I topped up my glass and took it with me, dripping juice all the way into my office.

~

My final class call took place just a few short weeks later. I emerged from my office feeling like I was in some kind of crazy time warp. Sunlight streamed through our living room, temporarily blinding me.

"Happy graduation!" Dom said, handing me a coffee. "How was your call?"

"Okay," I mumbled, being careful not to spill a drop as I plonked myself down on the couch. I hadn't officially graduated anything yet, seeing as I was still nowhere near publishing my book.

"Just okay?"

I sighed and shrugged a little. "The call was really good. I got a little emotional towards the end."

Dom turned his head to the side and jokingly pulled a face. "Nawww."

"It's just that… Well, I guess seeing everyone else finished with their books was hard. They shared their beautiful covers and blurbs, and I'm so excited for them; it was just… tough, I guess. I mean, I always knew I'd be doing it on a different timeline, and we had the move and everything…" I was mortified to notice a wobble in my voice.

Good grief, what was wrong with me this morning? I was so busy; I'd always known the book would have to wait a bit longer. I should be celebrating! No more classes or studying meant more free time for writing. It was all going to be perfectly fine.

So why didn't it feel that way?

I leaned back against the couch, closing my eyes.

For goodness sakes, I chided myself. *It shouldn't be this hard.*

From the second I'd discovered books, I only ever wanted to be an Author. I'd driven my parents crazy, aged three or four, constantly demanding, "What does *that* say?" as I pointed at the signs we drove past.

In my first week of school, I cried in frustration and disbelief that I couldn't yet read. But once I got the hang of that reading stuff, *man*, there was no stopping me. While all the other girls were on the netball courts, I was tucked up in a corner of the library reading stories about girl detectives and the mysteries of the Bermuda Triangle or the pyramids of Egypt. I totally geeked out whenever a Readathon was announced and thought Librarians had the coolest job in the world.

In High School, I convinced girlfriends to co-write stories with me and spent hours drafting plot outlines and drawing book covers with our names on them. I wrote poetry in every spare moment and was only ever early to English Literature class.

I'd always loved writing. I'd written soul-searching articles in the past. It should only get easier with time, shouldn't it?

From the very beginning of this project, a mantra from one of my online mentors ran through my head: "If you can write a blog post, you can write a book". I'd repeated this over and over. It'd helped immensely to cheer me up as I faced the overwhelming enormity of the task at hand.

It was only a heartbeat before I realised that writing a non-fiction narrative wasn't *quite* that simple. While my book class had covered all sorts of launch aspects and tips for writers of standard non-fiction books, it hadn't specifically covered creative writing or memoir. If I was going to write this book in story form, I was going to need more help.

Bingo!, I thought, making a beeline for our bookshelf. There was one book in particular I'd had since I was a teenager. It was a book on writing by a world-famous author. I'd carried it with me from house to house, setting it on each new bookshelf as a reminder of the biggest, scariest life goal I'd ever had.

I ran my fingers over the cover that I'd lovingly wrapped in clear vinyl more than twenty years earlier. Flipping through the pages, all yellowed by time, I felt my spirits lift. This book of wisdom held the answers, I was certain of it.

It was time to crank up the dial on my imagination, and let it run wild with the possibilities. It was time to get the hell out of my own way. Class may have been over but the work had only just begun.

EIGHT

I was thirteen-and-a-half years old the first time I decided I'd like more pocket money for clothes, cassette tapes, and velvet scrunchies. There was a small shopping complex I could walk to from our house if I allowed forty-five minutes or so. Not really understanding how these things worked, and in a surprising act of bravery for a timid young girl, I decided I'd just go into every shop there and ask them if they needed any help.

The video rental store was my first choice. Secretly I hoped I might also get a discount on my favourite movies and crunchy snacks. When the manager dismissed me, waving me away, I marched into the gift store, the chemist, the record store, and the newsagency.

Fresh out of luck, I sat on the parking lot kerb wondering how on earth the grown-ups did it.

I was just about to give up and head for home when I was hit by a stroke of pure genius. What was my favourite thing in the world besides books and movies? *Lollies!*

There was a deli in the complex that not only offered thinly-sliced cold meats and an extensive range of fancy cakes, but also a huge counter full of every kind of lolly a kid could imagine. They were the pick-and-mix kind that you could spend an age choosing with the fifty-cents of pocket money you'd earned by doing the dishes or cleaning your room.

Excellent!, I thought, jumping up to head back through the automatic double doors. Worst case scenario, if they didn't want to hire me, at least I could get myself a bag of lollies to soothe my sorrows on the walk home.

To my surprise and utter delight, the owner nodded that yes, actually, they *did* need someone to help out and that I could come in for my first shift that very weekend. I still bought a bag of lollies, but now it was to celebrate.

By the time I turned fifteen, I'd made a new school friend who mentioned that she was making more per hour working the counter of a local fast food restaurant and that she'd happily get me an interview.

The minute they told me I'd secured the job, I

skipped over to the deli to hand in my first resignation. I'd still work there until they found someone else, of course; I was so grateful to them for giving me my first job when no one else wanted me. But I was thrilled with the idea of moving up from a job where I spent more time mopping up floors than counting out sweets, to one with the glamour of uniforms and an actual *drive-thru*.

I smiled at the memory as Dom and I drove past that very same shopping complex more than twenty years later. I hadn't been back to this area in years. We were on our way to a restaurant in the hills to meet my family for lunch and celebrate Mum's birthday. The restaurant was located in a huge botanical park that came alive with tulip festivals during the spring, and picnics and live music throughout the summer months.

Our tyres crunched on the gravel as we drove up the long, winding driveway. Native bushland on one side contrasted perfectly with the manicured gardens on the other.

I spotted my family getting out of their car just as we pulled up nearby.

"Hi guys!" I called, as we jumped out of the car to hug them hello. "Happy Birthday, Mum!"

"Shall we go walk around the gardens first?" My Step-Dad suggested, leading the way.

My sister and my teenage nephew fell into step behind him, while my ten-year-old niece ran ahead of us all.

The weather was cool and overcast, perhaps explaining why the park was unusually quiet. Recent rains had resulted in a babbling brook and large muddy patches, making everything fresh and green. Birds chirped away happily in the treetops.

It felt like we were the only visitors there until we reached the main lawn, where we spotted a smattering of vintage Rolls-Royce cars. Sweeping curves and shiny chrome gleamed in the sunshine. Dom and my Step-Dad wasted no time running over to ask the owners all the details about all the things, and whether or not they really needed to own their own Rolls-Royce in order to join the club.

Being a Sunday, I couldn't help but think about how hungover I might have been in the past. How I wouldn't have enjoyed this walk at all; counting down every second until we could have wine with lunch. Instead I felt completely at peace in the moment, laughing with my family who were telling jokes and posing for photos. It blew my mind how I'd previously believed sobriety would be boring. That feeling of peace and complete relaxation never, ever got old.

As we reached the restaurant and walked inside, a woman bustled past carrying a stack of plates, doing a double-take as she recognised Mum.

"I know *you*," she smiled. "Is that you, Maria?"

Apparently they'd worked together in the past. As they started chatting and catching up on who they'd seen lately and what had happened to so-and-so, I wandered over to the dance floor. With Mum's help,

I'd hosted my twenty-first birthday party in this very same restaurant, even hiring a bus to transport everyone so they could drink with me and not have to worry about driving themselves home.

Wanting the day to last as long as possible, I decided a lunch event would be the best idea. Wearing a new, cherry-red lace top and my hair cropped into a shorter version of *The Rachel*, I had a blast. But, as per my usual programming, I drank too much, continuing on the bus ride home.

Later that night, my boyfriend and friends went out dancing, but by that stage I'd already gone to bed in a sorry state. I spent the next morning sobbing, distraught that I hadn't gone out with them afterwards; imagining that I'd cut the day short and would never have that much fun in my life ever again.

I hated my job at the time and didn't have any hobbies, interests or passions to pour myself into. Instead my passion was poured straight down my throat. My social life was the only place I derived any ounce of fun. I couldn't fathom that people actually felt pleasure or fulfilment from their chosen careers.

Even in my most recent corporate job, I was horrified at the thought of people who didn't drink, often waving my drink around the pub and wailing, "It would be like every day was a *weekday!*", to the great amusement of my colleagues.

Not once did I stop to consider what was so wrong with my weekdays that I was so eager to escape them. Never did I stop to think about how I could make my weekdays better instead of using booze as a crutch.

Now I was desperately trying to channel all my passion into this new career I cared about, even if it did mean working eighty hours a week to avoid working forty for someone else.

I'd been so nervous about taking a whole day off, worried I'd fall even further behind, but spending time with family and being in nature was just what the Doctor ordered. Re-energised and determined, I was ready to power my way forward.

~

"What are you doing?" Dom said, sneaking up on me as I was staring into my laptop screen a few days later. "I thought you were meant to be writing?"

"I'm learning!" I informed him, quickly closing my browser window.

Dom chuckled and put his hands on his hips. "Uh huh," he joked, raising one eyebrow. "*Please*, Little Miss Procrastinator, tell me *more.*"

"I'm not!" I argued, crossing my arms as he laughed at me.

"Okay, okay," I giggled, holding my arms up in surrender. "Maybe I am. It's just… I feel like I don't know enough yet."

"Come *on!*" Dom said, swivelling my chair playfully. "I've submitted the forms and purchased the barcodes. Now you just need to write an actual *book.*"

"Fine!" I laughed.

As Dom turned to walk out of my office, I tried for that ever-elusive nonchalant tone I was still yet to master. "Oh hey, so…"

Dom looked back. "What's up?"

"I received an email earlier. Well, an invitation really," I told him. Actually, more like the Universe's crazy idea of a double-dare.

"Uh huh," Dom nodded, waiting for me to go on.

"To give a talk at a wellness festival in a few months. Sasha Reid is organising it. You remember her." Dom nodded. "She also asked if we'd like to host a stall at the event, and suggested that we could use it for a book signing if we wanted? Or something like that." I mumbled the last part as I felt a deep blush expand across my cheeks.

"Hey *hey!*" Dom laughed. "That sounds great."

"It does," I nodded. "Only… it's less than four months from now, and we'd have to have the book completely published and have paperbacks ready to take with us. I mean, is that even do-able?" I held my breath as I waited for his answer, part of me hoping he'd tell me it was impossible. Not only would we have to work like mad to get it done in time, but there'd be so much more at stake. I wouldn't be able to back out if I said yes; I wouldn't want to let Sasha down. And if I was honest, even the *thought* of potentially failing so publicly made me feel ill. Was I *that* committed to this book? *Really truly?*

"Yeah, I think it is," Dom said finally. "It'll be a tight schedule, for sure, but I'm sure we can do it." He smiled. "We've done harder things before, right?"

"I guess so," I said, although I really didn't know. A bubble of fear and anxiety expanded inside me. Never mind the fear of public speaking that I was still working on, but *holy moly*, was I ready to crank things up this far? Was my writing even good enough?

Dom interrupted my thoughts. "If it was easy, everyone would do it," he shrugged and walked out of the room. It was a saying that had kept us going through the scariest parts of working for ourselves. Coincidentally, it was also a mantra that had comforted me on those heartbreaking days in early sobriety when it had felt insanely unfair that I was being challenged to stop drinking when no one else was.

The truth was, sobriety felt hard because it was *supposed* to. The gut-wrenchingly difficult days were the ones that had impelled me to truly grow and heal. The toughest parts of any journey changed and strengthened us the most.

"Hey, let's go somewhere," I called after Dom. Wherever my moxie was, it sure as hell wasn't sitting here reading research articles.

"Huh?" he called from the other room. "Like where?"

I smiled mysteriously. "You'll see."

"Well?" Dom said as we climbed aboard the city-link bus.

"Let's go check out the venue; see what we're dealing with."

I figured that if I saw the inside of the venue and became more familiar with it, I'd feel more confident about the whole thing.

Sasha's email mentioned that the event would be held at The Perth Town Hall. I'd never been there before but as we stepped inside and walked up the grand staircase, it was just as I'd imagined. Our footsteps echoed around the high ceilings and historic walls. Plaques and memorabilia lined every inch of the place, displayed in glass and wooden boxes designed to be seen but never touched.

Dom and I followed the signs to the main hall on the first floor. A few people milled about nearby, chatting in small groups or wandering in and out. Both doors were wide open and we stepped inside. The hall was massive with tall, narrow windows lining the walls. On the far side was a huge stage.

Turning slowly around the room, I attempted to take it all in, imagining myself up on that stage in front of the largest crowd I'd ever spoken to in my life. My stomach flip-flopped with nerves just thinking about it. A small stage in a dark nightclub was one thing; this was quite another. This could all go so horribly wrong.

What if I froze? What if I invited people to come to the book signing but then I didn't make it in time?

What if I failed spectacularly in full public view?

Some small part of me whispered, *What if this was exactly who you were meant to become?*

Deep down, below all of my fears and insecurities, I could feel it. There was a little swirl of excitement there. *What if, indeed.*

"If we're really doing this," I said to Dom, thinking out loud. "We'll have to go *all* in. I'll have to stop trying to run three different websites, and also stop taking on any new clients. Which means we'll have much less money - if any - for things like exercise classes, movie dates, or coffees out."

Our life savings were almost gone. The revenue from our online programs and Dom's clients would barely cover our ongoing business expenses. To cut off a large part of my income - to stop taking on private clients altogether - would be raising the stakes entirely. I wanted to be sure that Dom was completely onboard with what this meant before we said yes.

As opposed to my standard operating procedure of 'more is more', I'd long suspected that Dom actually enjoyed the challenge of depriving himself of things. "Let's do it," he confirmed with a cheeky grin.

The swirl of excitement did a pirouette around my stomach. The challenge was on.

Just then an elderly man carrying a broom strode towards us. He wore a navy jumper with what looked to be a volunteer logo on it. I smiled, eager to see if he wanted to chat about the building and its history.

He didn't smile back. "Can I help you?"

"Oh, hi," I said. "We're giving a presentation at an event here soon and just wanted to take a quick peek at the venue."

"Well we're closed to the public!" he barked, practically shooing us out with his broom.

"Oh… sorry…" I stammered, backing away. "But… the doors were open…"

Dom grabbed my hand and we beat a hasty retreat. Before I knew it, we were out on the street.

Dom looked at me and laughed. "Well, that went well."

I rolled my eyes and laughed with him. "Oh well, I saw enough of it, anyway. Let's get to work."

I was already having all kinds of new ideas. We'd need a poster for our booth, of course, and little 'thank you' cards to place inside the books. Plus I'd need to actually write a presentation talk. And finish the book, of course. Just because I hadn't had a chance to visualise myself signing books in the venue didn't mean it wasn't destined to happen.

As we rode the bus home, I knew that what was true in sobriety was true now. Everything I'd ever wanted was on the other side of fear. And the biggest miracle I'd need to get through this, was the miracle of self-belief.

NINE

Striding back to my office, I knew what had to be done. In a perfect world, I'd be able to drop everything else and bury myself in this writing project until it was done. But real life didn't work like that. There might never be a perfect day, or long stretch of quiet time, to sit down and write this book. I was going to have to get creative. I'd just have to do what I could, when I could, with what I had, and focus firmly on progress over perfection.

I'd once read: 'You can move ten things forward one step, or one thing forward ten steps'. I loved that concept. The way I'd been working wasn't sustainable, that was for damn sure. If I closed my eyes and allowed myself to imagine a single business focus, I felt overwhelmed with relief. I still wasn't sure if I was ready to be known exclusively for sobriety, but deep down I felt that this book was worth pouring all of my love and attention into.

Now, how would a successful Author behave?, I thought, psyching myself up to keep going. Becoming a minimalist in my home environment was one thing. As much as it pained me; as hard as I found it to let go of things, I was going to have to become a minimalist in my work too. I'd have to commit to a level of restraint and discernment I hadn't used before.

All fired up, I decided to start with my inbox. Switching on my laptop, I spent the next hour unsubscribing from the hundreds of newsletters I'd opted in to. No amount of research, or scrolling through social media, or distracting myself with admin tasks, would get this done. There was a time for learning and education, and there was a time to get busy creating.

Opening my to-do list, I archived all the draft posts and ideas I had for new blog posts and newsletters for my wellness and business sites. I crafted an email telling our subscribers that going forward, my focus would be on sobriety only.

As I clicked 'send', a bittersweet mixture of fear and nostalgia threatened to drown me. My recipe site had been my first creative baby; the direction that had drawn me out of the comfort of my previous career.

But I couldn't do everything. At least, not at once.

Pulling my calendar off the wall, I started brainstorming. If I could write the first draft in April, maybe I could write the second draft in May, edit in June, and maybe - just maybe - launch in July. That would give us just enough time to order a box of paperbacks to take to the event in August.

It was an insanely optimistic plan, for sure, but hadn't we done seemingly impossible things in the past when challenged by a big deadline? Heck, hadn't the past two years of sobriety proven that I could do all kinds of hard, previously unimaginable things when I applied myself?

Closing down every open window on my laptop, I opened my writing software. Once again, the cursor blinked, goading me. *Any time you're ready, lady.*

I thought about a Jedi mind trick I'd always loved to get myself to the gym, where I'd think, 'I'll just do ten minutes.' Once I actually got my butt there, I always did more than I expected.

So just write for ten minutes, I told myself. *Then you can have a break; maybe even a reward.*

Now, that was a cheery thought. If treats and rewards helped me through the hard work and milestones of early sobriety, they sure as hell could help me through the hard work of a mammoth creative project like this.

~

"Okay, so, the cover," Dom said, over breakfast the next morning. "What were you thinking?"

Holy moly. I'd always known that Dom would design the book, but I really wasn't ready to think about that just yet. I was still trying to wrap my head around how I'd manage to actually *write* the thing.

Scrunching up my nose, I tapped my spoon against my forehead. "Well... something cool. Like, a really unique graphic or something, I suppose. Not a photo."

"I'll make it look more like a graphic, yes, but I think it should be a photo of you," he said.

I groaned. "It doesn't have to be."

"It's *your* story, it should be a photo of *you*," he insisted.

My inner fifteen-year-old slumped her shoulders in silent protest. "Well... definitely not one of those cheesy close-up photos that the politicians have."

Dom looked at me. "What's wrong with a close-up?"

I shook my head. "No No *Nooooo*. Definitely not. Nobody wants to see a huge close-up of my head."

Dom threw his hands up, exasperated. "Not this again!"

We'd been down this road before. The first time he'd suggested putting my photo onto the home page of my wellness website, I'd lost the plot. We'd had a huge argument about it that had ended with me going to bed sobbing. That was back when I was still drinking; back when I didn't want to look under the hood at any of my insecurities or reactions.

I may have been upset when I went to bed, but by

the time I woke up, I was furious. *Why the hell was I arguing over this?*, I fumed all morning. *It was my website and I would do as I damn well pleased!*

In the end, after many strong words, we reached a compromise, and neither of us could comprehend why my reaction had been so severe.

Why did *I react that way?*, I wondered now. *What was so scary about having my photo on something?*

An unwelcome memory pushed its way into my consciousness. Throughout childhood, one of my favourite things in the world had always been experimenting with outfits, just for the fun of it. One day, I made the fatal mistake of wearing one of these colourful, flamboyant outfits to school. We lived in a low-income area where it was never a smart idea to stand out or paint a target on your back.

It was 1985. Channelling a cross between Cyndi Lauper and Madonna, I wore a fuchsia top with ruffles on the sleeves. My black and fuchsia checkered knit skirt skimmed the fuchsia tights at my shins, while a white, vinyl belt hung low around my ten-year-old hips. Big white earrings and a fuchsia bow in my hair completed the look.

I thought I looked so cute as I left the house. It didn't take long for the most popular girls in school to hunt me down. At morning recess they cornered me in the school yard, standing so close I could smell the bubblegum on their breath.

With a viscous sneer, the ring leader looked me up and down. "What are you *wearing?* Why are you wearing *that? Ewwww,* you *love* yourself, don't you!"

The other girls elbowed each other and sniggered. I wished with all my heart for the planet to swallow me whole right there. Instead I had to suffer their taunts for the entire day.

I was quiet and tearful as I arrived home from school, but I was too ashamed to tell my Mum or sister what happened. Some small part of me worried they'd laugh at me too.

How often are we made to feel small by others; taught to remain in our place? Taught that being who we are is not safe.

How interesting that this childhood programming could continue to play out in my subconscious without even being aware of it. It was painful to dig around in this stuff but as I did, those old shackles started to loosen their grip just a little bit.

I still didn't want a great big photo of my face on the cover, but maybe, *just maybe,* I had a compromise in mind. "Okay, grab your coat, mister. I've got an idea. Let's go get inspired."

Dom looked up from his phone. "Hhmm?"

I smiled mysteriously and he smiled back, clearly relieved that I wasn't going to dissolve into a meltdown this time.

It was only once we were safely on the city-link bus that I told him where we were headed: straight to the shiny new library in the city. Not only could we research book covers, but I could also find more books that would help me with the craft of actually writing this thing.

I'd adored libraries my entire life but I was especially excited to see this one. It had been under construction for many months and was finally open to the public. Located in the centre of the city, it took us only ten minutes or so to reach it.

As the automatic double door slid open, my breath caught in my throat. Architecturally designed, the result was stunning, with warm, timber detailing, winding staircases, and huge sweeping windows. It was possibly the most beautiful library I'd ever been in.

Galloping up to the desk like the absolute geek I'd always been, I asked for the library card I'd pre-ordered online. When the librarian handed me a free calico book bag to go with my shiny new membership card, it was official. I was in love.

I hugged the bag to my chest as we started up the staircase and Dom chuckled as quietly as he could, shaking his head.

"We're in search of the Biographies section," I whispered, leading him straight to the second floor.

As we started our expedition, we came across a gorgeous, curved timber book shelf.

"Imagine *your* book, right here," Dom whispered, pointing at the top shelf.

"Imagine," I whispered, stifling a giggle.

Turning the corner, we found what we were looking for. There were books from politicians, rock stars, chefs, and athletes. Most of the covers had the exact photo I *didn't* want.

"Okay," I said, pulling books out to glance at their covers before hastily placing them back. "So, I still don't want a close-up photo of my head. But maybe a full-length photo might be okay. Maybe if I was sitting at a desk, or perched on a bench, or something?"

Dom nodded, thinking it over. "Okay. Yep, yep, that could work."

"I was hoping there'd be a heap of examples that I could show you as inspiration, but none of these are quite right." I picked up a couple more books from the shelves. "But I guess these have a full-body shot, at least, so maybe that gives you some ideas?"

I handed the books to Dom and he squinted at them, not saying a word. I wasn't sure if this was a good sign or not.

"Oh!" I said, as an another idea popped into my head. It was a design I'd doodled in my diary a few days before. "What if the cover was pale gold, with light leaks all around the sides, and there were these kind of bubbles rising up around me? And you weren't sure if they were champagne bubbles, but actually they were *joy* bubbles?"

Dom stared at me like I was from outer space.

Then, just as suddenly, he snapped his fingers the way he always did when he was hit by design inspiration. "I think I've got an idea."

TEN

Ben was due to arrive at 10:00am. It was already 9:00am and not only was I not ready, but we were no closer to having a final cover shot in mind.

"I feel like I should have some kind of prop," I called out to Dom as I untangled my curling iron in the bathroom. "So I'm not just standing there like a dummy. Like maybe flowers or something."

"I've got a better idea," Dom said, grabbing the car keys from the little metallic bowl in the living room. "Balloons. Back in a bit." He stopped to kiss me briefly before disappearing out the door.

I didn't have the time or energy to question it; I was simply grateful that he had an idea in mind. I'd been writing for weeks and was 46,000 words into the first draft. As much as I felt exhausted, I was also looking forward to this photoshoot. It would feel real then, surely. Once we had a cover shot, the imposter would leave the building and I'd start to feel like a *Real Author* with a *Real Book*.

I put the finishing touches on my make-up and shimmied myself into my chosen dress. There was never any question about what I would wear. It was the best dress I owned and we didn't have the budget to buy anything new. The fact that we'd bought the dress on sale to celebrate my first six months of sobriety seemed only fitting.

"I'm as ready as I'll ever be," I sang out to Dom when I heard him return. He appeared in the doorway holding two heart-shaped, helium balloons.

Just then, the intercom buzzed. "Be right down," Dom said, pressing the button as we bustled our way out the door with the balloons and a large bag full of make-up, hairbrushes, and a change of shoes.

Not only was Ben one of Dom's closest friends, he was also a budding photographer. He'd offered to take the photo as part of his mission to hone his craft.

"Balloons, hey?" Ben laughed as we met him out the front of our building. "Let's take my car. I've got all my gear in the back."

Climbing into his small car with our myriad of baggage, we pulled away from the kerb.

"So," Ben said. "Big day, huh Bex? Do you enjoy these shoots?"

"Not really," I admitted. "I get so nervous. But I love that we're doing this one with you. I feel like it'll be a lot more fun."

I'd commissioned only two shoots with photographers over the past few years to create photos I could use on my websites. Back then I was still drinking, and both times I'd been so nervous the night before, I'd gotten stuck into the vino, even though I swore I wouldn't. This would be my first shoot sober, without a hint of a hangover.

"Okay," Ben said as he pulled into a parking space. "I was thinking we'd start up near my work building. Unless you guys had other ideas?"

"Sounds great," Dom said.

The three of us piled out of the car and jostled on the footpath, gathering up the equipment. The nearby buildings had sprouted from the recent economic boom and there were lots of sleek industrial walls to choose from.

Unfortunately, Mother Nature hadn't gotten the memo that it was Photoshoot Day. Each new corner greeted us with increasingly stronger, almost comical, wind gusts. We howled with laughter at the calamity that ensued; my dress constantly flying up, my hair blowing into my face, the balloons bopping me on the head.

"Yeah, I don't think this is working!" Dom bellowed over the noise of the wind. "Let's go try around the other buildings over there."

The nearby buildings housed a new cafe. Being

a Saturday, and nestled amongst office buildings, the cafe was closed. We could see a handful of staff crowding around a bench inside. Hanging lights cast a lovely warm glow against the shiny steel and glass facade.

Immediately spotting the photographic potential, Ben motioned to me. "Maybe stand in front of this window, Bex."

I shuffled my way over to where he was pointing. With a ton of effort and a bit of luck, I managed to make my dress, hair and balloons behave.

Ben had just started snapping away when a man wandered out from the cafe. "Hi," he said, greeting us with a nod. "What are the photos for?"

"Um, I'm writing a book," I said, having a temporary out-of-body experience as I realised it was the first time I'd ever spoken those words aloud to a stranger. "And Ben here is taking the cover photo."

The man looked at us for a moment like he was making his mind up about something. "Come inside," he said finally, indicating that we should follow him. "We're closed but you can take some shots in here."

Thanking him, we followed him into the cafe, briefly greeting the other staff. The cafe was gorgeous inside. Sunlight bounced along black shiny surfaces and across exposed metal beams. Funky, geometric artwork and caramel coloured couches lined the walls.

Grateful to be sheltered from the elements, we continued the photoshoot. After the harsh wind outside, every moment in the warm, cosy cafe felt surreal and wonderful.

"Okay, let me just change a setting. One sec," Ben said, stopping to adjust his camera.

"No problem," I said, grateful for the break. All that smiling was so exhausting. I didn't know how models did it. I was so much happier behind a computer screen.

As Dom started to help Ben with something, I wandered over to a nearby counter, picking up a magazine that was sitting on top. It was one of those contemporary magazines printed in matte rather than high gloss, all pastel colours and soft, pretty designs. As I flipped through the pages, something caught my eye. "Oh my God!" I laughed.

"What?" Dom said, looking up from whatever he and Ben were doing.

"This article!" I exclaimed, holding it up to show him. "It's Kristy's. Kristy Anderson."

"Ha, cool!" Dom said. Kristy was a friend of ours; a fellow creative entrepreneur we'd done several collaborations with. I'd always known she was an aspiring writer, but I had no idea she'd been published in such a huge magazine.

I ran my fingers over her name in print, while goosebumps prickled the back of my neck. What were the chances? On *this* day, in *this* magazine, in *this* cafe.

When I'd studied health coaching, the school's founder had often talked about synchronicity. He promised we'd experience it for ourselves the more we walked the path that was our true calling. Back then, my imagination had been swept up in the magic of this idea; this concept. And now, here it was. The timing of it was uncanny.

"Come on," Dom said, snapping me out of my daydream. "We're heading across the road."

Bustling out of the cafe with all our gear, we thanked the owner again.

"Quick," he said, searching the counter for something. "Before you go, tell me the name of your book."

I hadn't officially told anyone yet; I wasn't even sure if it was the final title, it was just something that Dom and I had been playing around with. But as he handed me a pen and paper, I was sure. Feeling the warm glow of the cafe permeate my fingers as a huge smile spread across my lips, I wrote down the words for the very first time: *A Happier Hour.*

"Thank you so much!" I yelped once again as Dom pulled me out the door.

Across the road, we wandered through the side streets, searching for inspiration. After a few minutes, we came across a small alley with one huge wall painted black.

"Stop!" Dom called out. "Your dress and the balloon, they really pop against this wall."

I groaned. We'd talked about this before. *Drinking* memoirs generally had dark covers. I wanted this to be a memoir about *sobriety*, not about drinking.

"I know, I know," Dom said, reading my mind. "But it works. Trust me."

"Alright, let's try it," Ben nodded, pulling his camera out of its bag. Happy to be out of the wind for a while, I went along with it, reassuring myself that this was just an experiment. We could always find a prettier wall later.

I tried various poses as we attempted to catch the light while simultaneously trying to tame the balloons. I was just starting to enjoy myself when Ben stopped to look at his camera. "Hang on, two secs!" he called.

Dom and I looked at each other. Maybe Ben could see that this wasn't working after all.

Ben looked up. His face was beaming. "You guys, I think we've got it. I think we've got the money shot!"

"*Ooh,* show me!" I squealed, as Dom and I ran over to look at the camera. Ben clicked through a stream of photos and I could absolutely see it. Dom was right; the colour, the dress, the balloon, it really did pop. I loved it.

"Ben, we're taking you out to lunch, right this second!" Dom announced, cracking up as I clumsily attempted to pull them both into a big, messy hug.

~

The very first sober birthday I ever celebrated as an adult fell on Day 30 of my original sobriety experiment. Instead of my usual cocktails, champagne, and dancing-on-tables celebration, I spent the night on the couch, cuddling with Dom, eating fancy raw chocolate, drinking tangy mocktails, and watching an '80s flick. To my surprise, it felt utterly scrumptious.

My second sober birthday was the big one; the one that'd always loomed in the background, helping to motivate and frighten me into being sober in the first place. It was the day I tumbled into my forties.

I hosted my first alcohol-free birthday party that year. A million lightyears from the parties I'd hosted before, it was a casual, celebratory afternoon tea on the balcony that turned out to be surprisingly perfect.

And now, here it was: my third birthday as a sober adult. This time, after months of tap-tap-tapping away at my keyboard with this deadline in mind, by some miracle I'd actually finished an entire first draft of a book.

If I could keep this streak going, I'd forever be loving sober birthdays.

"Quick, take a photo of me!" I squealed to Dom, throwing him my phone and jumping in front of our bookshelf to pose with the printed manuscript. Oh how I adored that word. *Manuscript.*

As Dom snapped a photo, I was beaming. It'd been harder than I'd ever imagined, but I'd truly gone and done it. *Me*, the woman who could barely finish her own *sentences* once upon a time. It still didn't feel real.

"Maybe I should get some eye glasses," I babbled, delirious with excitement. "You know, really look the part." I'd read somewhere that a Real Book contained about 50,000 words. Since I'd just exceeded that seemingly impossible word count, clearly there was no other conclusion to be made. I was officially a Real Writer.

"Come on, birthday writer girl," Dom laughed. "Get your jacket. Let's go."

We drove to my favourite pancake place, and my body tingled with excitement the whole drive over. It occurred to me how nuts it was that I used to dull this feeling by guzzling champagne whenever I'd wanted to celebrate. This feeling was way too sublime, too precious, to wash away. I hugged my knees to my chest, thrilled I'd finally learnt not to rob myself of it.

We arrived to find the cafe buzzing with activity. Warm, early-Autumn sunshine streamed through the windows, and the smell of coffee wafted through the air, too good to resist.

As I looked around, trying to find us a table, I noticed something even more delicious. The cafe was packed with people tapping away on laptops, scribbling notes over breakfast meetings, and making phone calls. People doing things, meeting people, and making things happen - and all before 9:00am!

It reminded me of one of my clients who constantly marvelled that she now had time in the morning to actually *do* things. I loved that thought because of the freedom it inferred. That in living alcohol-free, we could choose to reclaim our mornings, and to start the day in a powerful way that resonates throughout the rest of our lives.

As Dom placed our order, I was still grinning like a lunatic, still in awe that I had what it took to write an entire first draft of an actual *book*.

We managed to find a cosy table in the back, and while we waited for our pancakes to arrive, I posted the photo of me holding the manuscript onto social media. Biting my lip, I wrote a caption under the photo, sharing that the finished book would be coming in July.

"*Eeep*, it's scary putting a deadline out there," I said to Dom, doing a weird little dance in my chair, and passing my phone to him. "But having a bit of public accountability will only help spur me on, right?"

"Right," he smiled as he read the caption, handing the phone back to me a second before a waitress placed our coffee on the table.

I stared back at my phone screen, wondering if humans really *could* do just about anything they set their minds to. Sobriety, health, happiness, writing. It was all there waiting for us when we finally learned to get out of our own way. Well, by golly, it had only taken 41 years, but it seemed I'd finally learnt to get out of my own way.

I had a ton of lunch dates planned with girlfriends over the next few weeks, and I couldn't wait to celebrate with them. I craved some fun before I knuckled down again. I was under no illusion that the second draft would be tricky, but I was positive that the first draft was always the hardest part.

As I pushed my phone back into my bag, I glowed with the knowledge that the worst was behind me. It would definitely all be smooth sailing from here.

ELEVEN

"Okay, so what's next?" Dom said over breakfast, many weeks later.

"Writing. Writing. And *more writing*," I said, ever the Drama Queen, waving my spoon around the room to further illustrate my point that there was so much writing I'd already done, and still so much more to do.

"Oh really?" Dom laughed. "And who's fault is *that?*"

I pouted, diving my spoon back into my breakfast. I'd thought myself so clever to have finished the entire first draft by my birthday. I'd held my breath as I watched Dom read the final pages, hoping he'd look up and tell me it was the most magical thing he'd ever read in his life. Or, at the very least, that it didn't suck.

"What do you call *this?*" he said, the second he'd finished reading.

"Huh?" I'd said, flabbergasted. This wasn't the reaction I was expecting at all. Wasn't this the book concept we'd talked about? Then again, it was Dom who often said, "You can't take your privacy back after you've given it away." Was he worried I'd said too much?

"This is not a story," he said, staring me down, clearly willing to chase the truth after me if that's what it took. "This is a mashup of blog and social posts."

"Ohhh," I mumbled, stepping backwards, trying to feel my way out of the room. It was so hot in here all of a sudden, and I really didn't want to hear what came next.

"Ohhh," he mimicked, laughing. "Oh indeed, missy. You're going to have to write most of this again."

He was right, of course. I'd wanted that word count so badly that in the end I'd figured any words would do. But if I was honest I knew I was only fooling myself. So much for the hard part being over.

That was weeks ago, and if I'd buckled down, I would've finished a second draft by now. Instead I'd thrown myself into a ton of other work, peppered with the occasional yoga class or lunch date with girlfriends. Starting all over again, and creating a new draft that was actually cohesive, had seemed far too monumental a task.

Dom watched me now, making a mess of my chia pudding. "What if I made your birthday present today?" he said finally, possibly feeling sorry for me.

Since we still weren't taking a wage, we'd decided not to exchange birthday gifts that year. At the time, I'd joked, "Maybe a new Author website can be my gift." Although once I stopped to think about it, I'd actually loved that idea.

"Ooh, yes please!" I said, dumping my empty bowl into the kitchen sink. "I'll go start a mood board of inspiration!"

"Later! I'll get started. You go write. You can play with Pinterest later."

"Oh, but…" I started to protest, and then remembered how much writing there was left to do. Not to mention all the other work required to design, publish, and actually launch this thing.

"Okay, okay," I nodded, heading for my office, raising my chin into the air as I imagined myself donning an invisible bonnet of maturity and professionalism. "Today, I write. Second draft, here I come."

~

One of my favourite thoughts to keep me company during the hours upon hours of keeping my butt in the chair, was imagining people's surprise when I finished the book. In my mind, I pictured friends

and family awestruck with wonder, remarking, "*Wow,
she's a stubborn little mule!*"

I wasn't exactly sure *why* I found this image so
highly amusing. Maybe it was because I believed it
was the opposite of my typical behaviour when I was
drinking, which was one thousand percent flaky.

Motivated by this thought, I started to write a little longer each day, and a little faster. Each morning,
I saddled up to my laptop like Rocky Balboa jostling
his way into the ring.

For so long I'd experienced a strong, deep resis-
tance to going into the darker places in my mind. The
flashbacks; the overwhelming emotions; I really, really
didn't want to go back there. And yet, as I continued
to write, a peculiar feeling began to take hold. The
deeper I looked inside at my most shameful secrets,
and the more I unloaded them onto the page, the
lighter I felt.

What if rather than causing *more* shame and pain,
writing down my story actually liberated me?

Soothed by the thought, I flexed my hands and
did a little arm stretch above my head. And then,
with *Eye of the Tiger* whirling through my head, I got
back in there. *Ding ding, Round Two.*

When I still hadn't emerged from my office many
hours later, Dom tapped on the door and opened it
gently, no doubt unsure as to what he'd find. Some
writing days went well and I was all smiles at the end
of the day. Other days, cranky that it hadn't gone as
well as I'd hoped, I was much less of a delight.

"Yawsit toing geetie?" Dom said.

I looked up from my laptop, not understanding him at all; still completely immersed in the memory I'd just visited. "Huh?" I said, my eyes slowly swimming into focus.

"I said, how's it going, sweetie?" Dom said, seemingly entertained by the mere state of me.

"Oh. Really good! Some days it feels like it just flows onto the page, y'know? Like, I'm so in the zone."

I was beginning to understand just how much I loved that feeling. How freeing it was to become so absorbed in the moment that all my anxieties melted away.

For the first time I noticed it was getting dark outside. "What time is it?"

"Almost dinner time. But I wanted to show you something first." Dom smiled and motioned for me to follow him out to the living room. I stretched my shoulders as I stood to comply.

There, in the corner of the room, on his computer screen, was a mockup of the book cover.

"Oh my God!" I breathed, hugging him quickly before going in for a closer look. "It's a real live book!"

"Well, it will be," he said. "Do you like it? I think I might still change the font a bit, and I might move this over here…"

"I love it!" I cheered, hugging him again. "Thank you. This is so exciting!" Seeing a milestone like this come to life made it feel all the more real.

Perhaps it was temporary insanity driven by the

excitement and the timing, or perhaps it was the Rocky theme song still blasting in my head, but when I shared the photo with our subscribers and friends on social media, I captioned the picture, "*A Happier Hour* is coming this July and I cannot WAIT to share it with you! x"

July. Two months from now. Surely that wouldn't be a problem for an athlete with steely determination like Rocky. No problem at all.

~

My phone buzzed and I jumped on it, thrilled to have a distraction. I'd been working on the second draft solidly for weeks that felt more like years. After being shut in like a recluse for so long, it was nice to receive a reminder that there was still a real world out there somewhere.

It was a text message from Mum. "You guys home? We wanted to drop in."

"Yes! Sounds great!" I messaged back, springing out of my chair to find a pair of jeans and a jumper. I'd fallen into the habit of wearing the most comfortable thing I owned while writing: an old tracksuit that had almost certainly seen better days.

I quickly changed and scrunched the embarrassing outfit into the back of the closet, before calculating how many days I'd worn it, and instead taking it to the laundry basket.

"My parents are on their way over!" I called out

to Dom who was working in the living room. I'd
only just started to brush my hair when the intercom
buzzed.

"Hi!" I sang as I buzzed them up, holding the
door open to wait for them. I heard the elevator doors
open a second before I could see them. "Come in," I
said, hugging them hello. "Were you in the city for an
appointment or something?"

"We had a few things to do-" Mum said.

"But we wanted to give you something," my Step-
Dad finished mysteriously.

I smiled and looked at their hands but noticed
they weren't carrying anything.

"Okay," I laughed. "Come sit down. Would you
like a coffee? Or a tea?"

"In a minute," my Step-Dad said. "But first…"
Reaching into his back pocket, he pulled out an envelope. "This is for you guys."

As he handed it to me, I saw that there were a few
notes inside; I couldn't tell how many. I looked back
at him, confused.

His eyes shone with warmth and his voice was full
of emotion. "For your books," he said.

Suddenly I remembered a conversation we'd had
a few days, or maybe even weeks earlier. My parents
had asked how much a box of paperbacks were, and
how many we'd need to take to the event. At the time,
seemed like they were just asking out of interest, and
I hadn't given it any more thought.

What on Earth.

As I looked down at the envelope in my hand, I couldn't help it. My eyes filled with tears.

I leaned in, hugging them both. "Thank you for believing in us," I said, my voice breaking halfway through as I started to cry. Dom and I hadn't been entirely sure how we'd swing the cost of those books.

The tears fell even faster as I remembered a chat I'd had a few weeks earlier with one of the very first women I'd helped with sobriety. Celebrating almost two years of sobriety, she told me she'd wanted to stop drinking well before then but said, "I just didn't believe I was worthy of asking for help."

Oh my God. Was that me too? It rarely occurred to me to ask for help, and for the first time I could see how I'd always shied away from receiving it. In my peculiar, mixed-up mind, perhaps it was another way of avoiding intimacy. Maybe I was scared that if people caught a glimpse of my vulnerability, they might see *all* of me.

Was that why I'd held myself back from working on this book too? A memoir wasn't like a fictional novel, where a story could be criticised but the Author could shrug it all off, given that it was purely make-believe. A memoir meant exposing our most human, shameful secrets to the world.

All the procrastination and illness and nonsense I'd experienced to this point, were they simply driven by my fear of being fully seen?

An hour or so later, as I hugged my parents goodbye, I committed to being braver. Fear would overcomplicate. It would cause me to get in my own way, procrastinate, and keep myself small. Love would keep it simple, and straight from the heart.

TWELVE

Writing like a woman possessed, I somehow managed to finish ten chapters of rewrites in the following two weeks. The remainder was within close reach. I was aching to get it done, but I was even more desperate for some time out. I missed my friends and what I remembered of my life. I'd been in the writing cave for so long, I worried I had completely forgotten how to behave in front of other humans.

My friend Diana was hosting a meditation retreat at her new home and I'd offered to give Zara a lift. She was already waiting for me in front of her apartment building when I pulled up. "Hi honey!" I called out the window, waving.

She saw me and bounced over, opening the car door and hopping in with a grin. "Thanks so much for picking me up!"

"No problem," I said. "I figured it's a long drive; it'll be more fun together."

Diana, recently inspired by a tree change, had moved with her love to a beautiful area in the hills. Funnily enough, it was an area very close to the high school Zara and I had attended. I adored it up there; all eucalyptus trees, kookaburras and kangaroos. It was like another world.

Almost an hour later, as we drove down one of the long, winding roads that looked like all the others, Zara pointed. "I think it's down here," she said, shuffling forward in her seat so she could get a better view through the windscreen. We were so deep in the countryside that we no longer had cell phone reception, and therefore no GPS. It was glorious.

"Yep, I think you might be right," I said, spotting a group of cars parked towards the end of the road. Pulling up to the kerb, we climbed out, just as another car parked next to us.

"Yoohoo!" the driver called and waved as she and her passenger exited the car. "Are you here for Diana?"

"We are!" I said. "Do you know which way?"

"I think it's just over here," she said, leading the way. In a single file, we followed her down a little trail hidden from the road, crossing an adorable wooden bridge, finally reaching the front door of Diana's home. Built from huge jarrah logs with high, exposed beams, the warmth from the pot belly stove burning in the living room was precisely what my soul craved.

Our guide quickly disappeared to talk to some of the other guests. Zara and I found Diana in the kitchen and hugged her hello.

"I'm so glad you guys came!" she said. "Help yourself to a tea or some snacks."

Lined across the huge kitchen counter were dozens of herbal tea blends, plates overflowing with bliss balls, and other yummy treats. From the kitchen, there was a stunning view of sunlight streaming through the surrounding trees full of wildlife. I never wanted to leave.

We just had time to make ourselves a cup of tea before Diana started rounding us up. "Okay ladies, if you'd like to come into the living room and grab yourself a chair or cushion, we'll get started."

Zara and I shuffled in as the twenty or so women found themselves a place.

"Those seats might be a bit warm," Diana whispered to me, indicating the seats closest to the stove. Zara and I looked at each other and I could tell she was as unfazed as I was. On this cool winter's morning up in the hills, the thought of getting toasty in front of the fire was absolutely scrumptious.

"Perfect," I said, plopping myself down.

Diana introduced a woman who led us through a deep meditation exercise, and I realised how shallowly I'd been breathing lately in my rush to get everything done. As I slowly allowed myself to relax, in a collective breath with so many other women, the feeling was sublime.

Afterwards, we all lingered, not wanting this experience to end.

Diana was the first to stand. "If anyone would like to stay for another cup of tea and a chat, please feel free."

I turned to Zara. "Are you in any hurry?" I sure wasn't.

"Nope," she giggled. "Actually, I was going to ask if you wanted to grab lunch nearby before we head back?"

"Brilliant! Shall we ask Diana if she wants to come with?"

Zara nodded and we made our way into the kitchen to make another cup of tea. Heading outside to the large wooden deck, we found Diana chatting with another woman she introduced as Celia.

"And Bex is about to be an Author!" Diana said. "She's writing a book!" Her voice shone with pride and I adored her for it.

"How wonderful!" Celia exclaimed. "What's it about?"

Oh God. I still didn't feel confident that I wouldn't choke on this part. Thankfully this stranger had a cup of tea in her hand rather than a glass of wine.

"Uh. It's about my journey to sobriety." I willed my body not to betray me but I could already feel the scarlet blush creep up my chest and across my cheeks.

It always seemed to go one of two ways whenever

I blurted that out. Most often, the way was awkward. She stared at me as I racked my brains trying to think of a great way to change the subject.

After a long moment, she nodded. "That's so brave!" she finally said, her face beaming like sunshine.

"It's *so* brave," Diana agreed. Part of me squirmed with warm gooey love at this, while another part of me did everything in its power to not grab her by the arm and wail, "*Brave how? What could happen? What?*"

"I'd love to read it," Celia said. "Diana, will you tell me when it's out?"

Another woman came over to talk to Diana and Celia, which we took as our cue.

"Lunch?" Zara and I whispered to Diana, gesturing down the hill, hoping she'd understand our invitation.

"Next time," she smiled before hugging us goodbye.

There was an amazing cafe located just a few tree-lined streets away. Happily, it was the exact place Zara had in mind, thanks to their decadent, gluten-free slices, superfood smoothies, and creamy coconut curries.

The cafe was not dissimilar to Diana's new home. Constructed entirely of large, jarrah logs, it was perched high on a hill, with tree tops and birds visible from every window.

The last time I'd been there, the owner, Bethany, had recognised me from the recipe blog I wrote many moons ago; the one I'd closed down in order to write the book. She was warm and funny, and when Zara and I arrived, I was thrilled to see she was working that day.

She spotted me a split-second after I saw her. "Rebecca! Hello!" she called, coming out from the back of the kitchen with a huge smile.

"Hi! This is my friend, Zara," I told Bethany.

We started chatted about her beautiful cafe and food before Bethany said, "Oh and Rebecca! I saw on social media that you've been writing a book and I had an idea that if you wanted to have a book signing here, we could organise one together?"

Bethany's cafe often hosted local artists and musicians and I could totally see it, thrilled with the idea of launching the book in such warm and cosy surroundings. "Oh, what a wonderful idea, thank you! That sounds amazing!"

"Okay then, so we'll talk," she laughed, coming around the counter to hug us.

A waitress appeared, and grabbed two menus from the front counter. As she showed Zara and I to an empty table, I marvelled at how the more we put ourselves out there, the more we crossed paths with people who wanted to help and co-create with us.

Two hours and many scrumptious morsels later, as Zara and I started the long trek home, we got to talking about how therapeutic writing was; how it could help to make sense of the baggage we carry around for far too long. How it helped to make peace with our past so we could move forward. And how much suffering came from clinging to our old identities.

For so long after I stopped drinking, I kept trying to fit myself into my old life and identity. When friends invited me to big, boozy affairs, I told myself I had to go, and dreaded every second leading up to it.

Over time, and with the book to write, I'd started saying a loving 'no, thank you' to events that didn't make my heart giddy with excitement. In turn, it had created more space and energy to attend events like Diana's, where I'd met a bunch of amazing soul sisters, shared deep and meaningful chats, deep belly laughs, and delicious food. And later, driving home, I felt completely filled up.

It's okay to change, I reminded myself.

For the first time I saw the correlation throughout life, whether in work or socially. That finding the courage to say no to the things that don't truly light us up, liberates us to say yes to more of the things that do.

~

After a multitude of writing sessions that felt like they ached deep within my bones, the third draft of the book was finally done. Many months before, my friend Sophie had given me a gift voucher for my birthday. It was for a three-course dinner for two at a Thai restaurant nearby. We'd been saving it ever since, waiting until we had something big to celebrate. Finishing the third draft felt like the perfect reason.

"Shall I dress up?" I asked Dom as he called to make a reservation.

"I've been past this place before," he replied, waiting for the restaurant to pick up. "It's pretty casual. But go for it, sweetie, if you feel like it."

I wanted to. After weeks of writing alone in my office wearing the same old tracksuit pants we couldn't yet afford to replace, I was dying to wear something pretty. I was starting to not even feel like a *woman* anymore.

I *so* wanted to feel beautiful and dress for the special occasion and celebration that it was. Only, I was also dog tired, and aching for rest, and just wanted to be comfortable.

I sighed, settling on jeans and a sparkly green jumper.

"Let's go," I said, meeting Dom at the front door.

Thankfully the restaurant was very casual, with bright red carpet and faux-gold bric-a-brac adorning the walls. Inside the front door was a long counter. The wall above displayed a number of Gold Plate Awards they'd won many years earlier. It always intrigued me when restaurants displayed their long-ago achievements like this. It always begged the question: what had gone wrong more recently?

Being a Friday night, almost every table was full of people happily chattering away. Hungry and exhausted, we ordered as quickly as possible.

"To the third draft," Dom said, raising his glass of coconut water after it arrived.

"Hurray and cheers," I smiled, clinking my glass against his.

We sat in silence, waiting for our meals.

"It's loud," I said finally, as the voices around us began to climb to a dull roar. Dom nodded. I tried to think of something else to talk about, but I was way too exhausted to speak. One look at Dom and I could tell he felt exactly the same way. So much for our romantic night out. I met his eyes and we both managed a small laugh at the madness of it all.

"I'd give anything just to lie down on this floor right now," I joked.

"Yes!" Dom laughed. "I'm wiped. How about we skip dessert and have something at home instead?"

"Deal," I said, knowing I'd barely be able to get through our main meal with my eyes open.

We'd have to be up at ridiculous o'clock the next morning to start the final edits, in order to meet this impossible deadline. The sooner we could climb into our soft, comfortable, delicious bed, the better.

THIRTEEN

Our monthly rent payment was due later that week. I attempted to breathe like a normal person while I opened the internet banking site on my laptop, but as I clicked to send our payment and saw what was left, my anxiety spiked.

So here it was. The moment I'd feared most. There was just two weeks rent left in our account, total, never mind money for bills or food. We had a tax bill we'd be forced to start paying in just a few days. Dom was in the middle of two big design projects for clients, but they wouldn't have payments due until at least the following month. The book was nowhere near finished. Even if I were to take on clients again and postpone the book, it wouldn't save us now; we were well past the point of no return.

I stared at our account balance, willing it to change. Forcing myself to think of *something*. We'd already sold everything we could. We'd even talked about selling our car to buy us more time, but had quickly scrapped the idea when we realised we'd end up spending more on public transport than we'd be able to get for an unreliable sixteen-year-old car.

Dom appeared in the doorway of my office. "How's it looking?" he asked, his face pulled into a grimace.

"Not good," I groaned. "Like, really not good."

Walking into the room, he perched himself on a chair. "Okay. So let's think," he said. "Could we take out a loan?"

I nodded as I fought back tears. I sincerely doubted a bank would approve us for a loan.

"Or… we could declare bankruptcy," I suggested, as casually as possible. "And close the business."

There was a long pause while Dom waited for my eyes to meet his.

"And do what?" he said. "Go back to the corporate world?"

"Well… yeah," I shrugged, too choked by emotion to say anything more.

"We're not giving up yet," Dom said, standing to walk away.

My hands were shaking as I attempted to move my mouse and close the banking window. I really cared about this work. I loved helping people, and working for ourselves, but how far did we have to go, really? If it wasn't working, it wasn't working. Was it really worth all this stress? Was it really worth working ourselves into the ground?

I thought about the carpark in our apartment building. Bizarrely, along one wall there was a large section of windows with a view into the office building next door. During office hours, we could always see people working away at their desks.

Many times we'd smiled as we'd walked past those windows, thrilled to have escaped our own corporate cubicles. But now, for a moment, I felt jealous of those employees. Envious of their ability to switch off when they went home and not have to carry the weight of their own business on their shoulders. Resentful of their paid annual leave, sick leave, and regular salary. Jealous that they could afford to buy new clothes when their old ones grew holes in them. But most of all, nostalgic for the way I'd stayed cozy in my comfort zone for all those years.

It's not giving up, I reassured myself as I shut my laptop. *It's just being realistic and knowing when to walk away.*

In a stupor, I sat staring at the wall for what felt like hours, until Dom reappeared in the doorway. He flashed his phone at me to show me a website open on his screen. "Okay," he sighed. "I guess we can have a look on the employment websites."

"Okay," I nodded, trying to be brave. A single

tear began to run down my cheek and I wiped it away angrily.

Taking the phone from his outstretched hand, I stared at the screen. I tried to motivate myself to type into the little search box, but I was paralysed.

All the crazy challenges we'd already overcome flashed through my mind. The insanely long hours, everything we'd sacrificed to get here, the number of people we'd helped. Was I really going to walk away now, never knowing what could have been? Was this how it was all going to end? *Really?*

We still had two weeks rent left, and possibly enough food still in our pantry to keep us going until then. If the absolute, very worst thing that happened was that we lost every cent of our hard-earned life savings and had to go back to the corporate world, at least I'd have a *book* to show for it. At least I'd have proven to myself that I could do it. At least all of this stress and struggle wouldn't have been for nothing.

I thought about a documentary I'd seen recently that featured an interview with a man who'd witnessed his friends perish in a plane crash.

"It changed everything," he'd said, his voice heavy with emotion. "Now I live like there's no tomorrow."

In the decades since, he'd let his passion guide him through life. This tragic, life-changing incident was the catalyst that had inspired him to pour his heart and soul into everything he did.

And I thought about what the term, 'Live like there's no tomorrow', used to mean to me. It was so superficial; to drink like a fish and forget the consequences.

Now it meant so much *more*. It represented living a conscious life, challenging myself, and finding joy in simple pleasures. Experiencing life, relationships and emotions with every fibre of my being.

I was well aware that one day there would *be* no more tomorrows - for each and every one of us. And when that moment came, I wanted to know in the depths of my heart that I had truly *lived*. I wanted to know that I had given it my all; that I had lived every day like it was the greatest gift on earth. Because it was.

Other people had dealt with much worse situations in life and bounced back from them. And so would we.

"Put it away," I said finally, handing Dom's phone back to him, my backbone making one final, glorious appearance. "We're not giving up yet."

~

With renewed focus, for the next two weeks we worked like never before. From dawn until deep into each night, Dom edited the book while I took his notes and painstakingly rewrote the entire thing, chapter by chapter, scene by scene, and finally, down to the very last sentence.

Before we'd started editing, Dom and I had sensibly and maturely agreed we'd compromise as we went, but between Dom's brutal honesty and my compulsion to fiercely protect my words, we butted heads more often than not.

"This phrase doesn't make sense," Dom said, more times than I could count.

"It does so!" I forever insisted. "It's *fine*. It makes perfect sense. People will get what I mean."

"What people?" Dom demanded, entirely unmoved by my apparently sensitive artistic temperament. "*I'm* people and I don't understand it."

I'd always known this challenge would push me to grow as a creative business owner, and as a human, in more ways than I could possibly imagine. I knew it would call me to walk my talk when it came to priorities, time management, tenacity and self-belief. Because it was all very exciting coming up with these big plans, and it felt heavenly, dreaming of the finished product. But the hours and hours of devotion required in between those two milestones? That was the part it all depended on.

One of my clients had once joked, "Nobody ever told me that running my own business would be a crash course in personal development!"

At the time I'd laughed and said, "*Aahhh*, but that's where the magic happens, my friend."

Somewhere in amongst the chaos of editing, I remembered that our payment processor had once offered us a working capital loan with no formal approval process required. At the time I'd ignored it as part of our 'no sinking into debt' policy, but this was no time to be precious. I hunted down the email and sent it off, crossing my fingers and toes that it would be enough to get us over the finish line. And of course, that we'd eventually be able to pay it back.

By the time we'd finished a fourth complete revision of the book, I felt like I was losing my mind. At this point we could both recite entire paragraphs. Words swam through my dreams until I wasn't sure I knew what words even *meant* anymore. Like when you say a single word over and over until eventually the whole word seems wrong; just a completely made-up set of letters that has no business thinking of itself as a real word. I was delirious.

Hoping against all odds we'd actually created something resembling a book, we sent a digital copy to my e-reader. Although my body screamed its deep desire to lounge on the couch, I got to work on the blurb and back cover copy while Dom braced himself for another full read-through. I prayed with every ounce of strength left in me that it would at least be *close* to the final version.

When I went to fetch a glass of water from the kitchen a few hours later, Dom was still glued to the device. From his seat on the couch, he tapped his foot back and forth against the rug. He seemed agitated, but I couldn't tell whether in a good way or a bad.

I stared at him, telepathically willing him to hurry up and give me the final verdict. Finally, he looked up. His face was still agitated, and still I couldn't read it. "Let's go for a walk."

"Okay," I said slowly. As I went to retrieve my coat, I braced myself. I was exhausted beyond recognition and really, *really* didn't want to hear that it needed another rewrite.

We rode the elevator down in silence. It was only when we were out on the street that he finally glanced at me.

"Well?" I said, warily, digging my feet into the ground, preparing myself for the worst.

"It's good," he said as he started walking, then turned his head to smile back at me. "Really good."

For a second I was sure my knees would give out beneath me, and I begged my ears to not be playing tricks on me. "Really?"

"Yep!" he beamed, his pace picking up. I ran after him, attempting to fall into step beside him. "There are a few bits that still need some last-minute tweaks, but..." He paused and looked over at me again. "I think it's just about ready."

My eyes filled with tears. I was so entirely knackered that I could only nod and smile. I felt like I'd conquered a mountain. It was the same kind of mountain I felt like I'd climbed in sobriety. The closer you got to the top, the more exhausted you felt. You felt like you'd been at it for so long. You started to wonder if it was all worth it; if maybe you'd come far enough. It was harder to breathe; harder to remember why you'd actually wanted it in the first place. And then - finally - you climb the final steps and reach the top. And the view was *glorious*.

It took so much time, energy and patience to get there. It was so tempting to give up before the magic happens. But it was only from the pinnacle that you finally understood you could do hard things. You could follow through. You were stronger than you'd ever imagined.

But it wasn't over yet. There was still the long climb back down the mountain.

We'd barely walked back into the apartment and slumped onto the couch when my phone buzzed. It was a text message from Jenna. "Hey chicky, want to meet for coffee tomorrow?"

Did I ever.

FOURTEEN

My former colleagues started work at 8:00am, and once in a blue moon the whole team managed to get out of the office for a coffee date. Today was one of those moons.

Jenna invited me to meet them at one of our favourite catch-up places. A fancy, boutique, inner-city hotel, it was located directly across the street from their office building.

Jumping off the city-link bus, I clicked my phone to check the time. *Phew! Minutes to spare*, I thought to myself, delighted to note that I was early for once.

As I hurried through the front courtyard, I couldn't wait to see them all. I was thrilled to have finally finished writing so I could give them my full attention.

Derek and Brian had beat me to it. Smiling and waving from their large mahogany table just inside the entrance, I grinned as I spotted them. Soft winter sunlight streamed through the front doors towards them, enveloping the entire room in a delightful haze. Fragments of light reflected off water glasses and chandeliers, while surrounding tables buzzed with small groups of people in suits, taking notes, and sipping coffee over morning meetings peppered with the occasional jaunty laugh.

"Hi guys!" I sang as I reached them. Jenna walked through the door right at that moment, just in time for me to hug her hello before a waitress appeared, ready to take our order.

I knew it was just a quick, casual coffee date but I'd dressed up for the occasion anyway, wearing my favourite navy, floral dress over tights, just for the fun of it. The skirt billowed around me, swept up by a random gust of air as I sat down. It felt heavenly to be part of the outside world again after months of writing alone in my room, and I silently begged time to slow down so I could enjoy every second of it.

Before the waitress had even returned with our coffees, Derek and Brian had us in hysterics, regaling us with stories of their latest home renovation escapades.

Jenna laughed as she shared her recent travel stories and adventures, "And that was the last time I'll ever go *there*."

Brian turned the conversation to me, "And Jenna tells us you're writing a book?"

"I am indeed!" I laughed and blushed. "It's actually so weird to be in this hotel," I paused, gesturing to the walls around us. "Because I just finished writing a scene that took place here. And I was *so* deep into the writing process that it feels like I was literally just here, you know? Such a bizarre and eerie feeling."

"And I can't believe you've almost finished it!" Jenna said, giving me a friendly little nudge me in the ribs. "That's so amazing. What's Dom doing today?"

"He's hard at work on the book interior design," I said.

"The interior?" Jenna said. "Oh wow. You never think about things like that when you buy a book; that someone would have to choose all those things."

"I know," I giggled. "Fonts, margin sizes, spacing. Who knew there was so much to think about?"

"Well, I can't wait to read it!" Derek announced, leaning back in his chair with a smile. "You'll have to come in and give us a signed copy so we can put it on the shelf at work."

Without a smidge of warning, my stomach violently lurched. Like I was on an elevator and my body had just plummeted down from the thirty-eighth floor while my stomach desperately attempted to cling to the floor we'd left behind.

On the outside, I was fairly sure I was smiling and nodding, but on the inside, I was somewhere in free fall.

I'd already shared part of my story publicly already, and I'd shared so much more inside the safety of our membership site, but for the first time it dawned on me that this would be taking things to the next level. This would be like handing every one of my previous colleagues a copy of my personal diary.

My mind raced through all the scenes in the book and all the drama I'd tried so hard to keep separate from my work life. I frantically tried to piece it all together; to make sense of how it could ever possibly co-exist. Explosions erupted behind my eyes as I visualised worlds colliding.

"Well, when you're ready," Jenna said, reaching out to touch my hand, evidently catching the look on my face.

As we finished up our coffees and gathered our coats, I tried to breathe normally, but the anguish was still there. My stomach was a jumble of fears and doubts. Was I ready for the entire world to know my inner most thoughts and feelings; to know my most shameful history?

And more than that, what if the book wasn't any good? My mind spiralled, imagining the worst. "*Oh dear, did you read it?*" They'd whisper behind my back, embarrassed for me and my terrible writing, tut-tutting at what an awful shame it was that I'd succeeded at stopping drinking, only to fail at my lifelong dream. Oh how they'd shake their heads over their morning coffee at the tragic story of a woman who'd shared something so shameful, only to have to face the very managers who'd read her entire diary when she was forced to return to the corporate world.

Out on the street, as I hugged everyone goodbye, I attempted another shaky breath. As I crossed the street, heading for my bus stop, my stomach suddenly changed lanes and I thought I might throw up. Up until now I'd naïvely believed that writing the book might actually be a way to reclaim myself from my past reputation. But what if it only made it worse? How awkward would these coffee dates - and all of my relationships - be, if this entire thing was a complete disaster?

~

I woke before dawn the next morning, although part of me was sure I'd never slept. My eyelids flew open a nanosecond before my feet hit the ground.

"What're you doing?" Dom mumbled, stirring slightly.

"Just fixing one last thing," I whispered, heading for the door. I avoided the wardrobe mirror, certain that I'd see a crazed look in my eyes.

"*Nooo*," Dom groaned, pulling a pillow over his head.

"*Yes*," I insisted, pulling a track suit over the top of my pyjamas. It was freezing outside. "I just want to change the wording on one last sentence."

Dom opened his eyes just in time to see me make

a run for my office and reached out to grab me by the waist. "No!" he roared, playfully pulling me back onto the bed; nuzzling his lips into my neck. "It's ready. It's time."

I giggled as my body relaxed into his, giving in, but only for a minute. Scurrying out of his reach like a mad woman, I dashed into the other room and to my laptop. "It's not ready! I can do better."

"*Please*," Dom called after me. "Just stop. You can put it in the *next* book. You could spend the rest of your life rewriting. You'll become a better writer every day and you'll still never be completely happy with it. Eventually you have to let go."

As I switched on my laptop, a heady mix of emotions threatened to strangle me. All choked up, I started to cry. I was beyond exhausted. I hadn't slept a full night in weeks. Some part of my mind insisted on clinging to consciousness while I tossed and turned every night, constantly rearranging words in my head.

I pushed myself to keep going, which only made the tears fall harder and faster.

As I stared out the window, I thought about an article I'd written months earlier, celebrating two years of sobriety. Since it was for a big publication - a global wellness site with a huge audience - there was some pressure involved, but that didn't explain why writing it felt excruciatingly difficult.

I wasn't happy with the finished story, but after weeks of playing around with it, and much huffing and puffing, I sent it off anyway.

Just when I'd accepted that it wasn't good enough to publish, I finally heard back from one of the site's editors. She liked the idea of the piece but suggested an extensive rewrite.

Grateful to receive a second chance, I tried again, slaving at it for days, and still I wasn't satisfied. I couldn't figure out why on earth it felt so ridiculously hard. When the editor's deadline arrived, I felt frustrated and slightly defeated, but I sent it off again.

Weeks later, just when I'd accepted that it truly was doomed, I heard back from the editor. They loved it and would publish it soon.

When I read the final piece online, my heart sank. Not only was I not proud of my writing, but I didn't like the additional lines that had been edited in. I was so close to not even sharing it with our subscribers and friends; all because of my fear of not being good enough.

Despite my reservations, the article was loved and well received, shared thousands of times. And all because I'd allowed myself to be vulnerable and to send my work out into the world even though, in my mind, it wasn't 'perfect'.

It was a stern lesson about fear and perfectionism then and it was a clear message now. Honesty and enthusiasm had the potential to help more people than any perfect sentence structure ever would. Sharing stories and standing in our truth gave others permission to do the same.

Done is better than perfect, I reminded myself, taking a trembling breath. Dom was right. It was time to wish the book well and send it off. If there was one thing I'd learnt during sobriety it was that true confidence came from taking *action*, one small, scary step at a time.

I'd hope for a lovely reception for the book, of course, but I was beginning to understand that I'd never be able to control anything outside of myself; nor did I need to. The only thing that truly mattered was that I lived a courageous life and finished what I'd set out to do.

FIFTEEN

Dom and I spent the next few days in lockdown, existing solely on packet soups and toast as we put the finishing touches on the book files before uploading them to our chosen distributors. It was well after midnight on the third night when we were finally done. Too exhausted to muster an ounce of enthusiasm for a high-five, we fell into bed like comatose zombies.

We'd been in bed for what felt like seconds when Dom stirred beside me, reaching over to retrieve his phone from the nightstand. Resigning myself to another night lost to insomnia, I held my eyes tightly closed, willing sleep to come for me; sensing it was still dark outside.

"Oh shit!" he said, pulling back the bed covers and jumping out of bed.

My heart skipped a beat. "What is it?"

Dom tossed the phone across the bed while he rushed to get dressed, pulling his jumper on backwards. I rubbed my eyes, attempting to read the blinding white screen in the darkness. On his phone was an email from our US distributor.

My eyes grew wider as I read the subject line: *'FILES REQUIRE YOUR IMMEDIATE ATTENTION.'*

Quickly scanning through the email, I saw it was mostly technical jargon that only Dom would understand, but one line stood out: *'does not meet our submission requirements.'*

Oh crap.

I continued scanning: *'contains elements that extend beyond the trim line and may be cut off during the production process.'*

Double crap.

I still wasn't sure I completely understood the message, but I had to assume anything being 'cut off' couldn't be good. Stumbling out of bed, I headed for the shower. I could hear Dom switching on his computer in the living room and filling the coffee pot.

By the time I'd emerged from the shower, Dom was in a trance-like state, staring at his computer screen, frantically attempting to fix the files. I helped as best I could by pouring coffee and topping toast with peanut butter.

I'd always loved that our living room faced east and was flooded with light every morning. The sunrise was just starting to make its magical appearance on the horizon beyond the city skyline.

As I stared at the view, sipping my coffee, I thought about all the sunrises I'd witnessed on my way home from parties; all those dawns I'd spent so desperately trying to keep the party going. How I'd always mourned daybreak as a symbol of something dying. Now it symbolised new life.

"All done," Dom nodded, finally stopping for breakfast. "And now we wait for approval." He crunched into his toast, spilling crumbs down his t-shirt, before plopping himself onto the couch.

And wait we did, checking our inbox every five minutes for an email that never came.

The next morning, when we woke from yet another short, shallow sleep, there was still no word. We were one day closer to the event and still not able to launch.

We moved through the morning like we were underwater, stunned by the excruciating slowness of time. Finally, just after 11:00am, Dom whooped as he checked his email, punching his fist in the air.

"Yes?" I said, hope and excitement filling my chest. He passed his phone over so I could read it: '*Congratulations! Your interior and cover files meet our technical requirements for printing. The next step is to order your proof copy.*'

"*Whoohoo!*" I yelped, doing a crazy little jig on the

spot, overcome with glee.

"Okay, let's order it," Dom said, clicking his mouse to wake his computer, his face completely lit up. "I'll get the U.S. copy delivered via express shipping." After placing that order, he quickly requested a proof copy from our Australian distributor as well. We expected the Australian copy to arrive within a few short days. We could only hope that the U.S. copy would arrive just as quickly.

"Time to share it!" Dom hollered, holding his phone so close to my face that I could practically kiss it, words swimming before my eyes.

I pushed my head back into my pillow to read the news we'd been waiting for. In addition to the paperback versions, our ebook versions had now also been officially approved.

We hadn't yet received the physical proof copies but at this point, they were merely a formality. I mean, how bad could they be?

"It's launch day!" I giggled, jumping out of bed. I was keen to shower and eat breakfast before we started sharing the news. I wanted to wade around in the anticipation for a little while. Part of me still couldn't believe this day had finally arrived.

This it it, I repeated over and over in my mind, humming a joyful ditty as I dressed.

Goosebumps travelled up and down my arms as

we shared the news with family and friends and on social media. I could barely stop the tears from flowing as people started commenting and messaging back, saying how happy they were for us and how excited they were to read the book.

When a few enthusiastic readers sent photos of themselves with the ebook on their phones and tablets, I felt overwhelmed with gratitude that I hadn't given up. I would have missed out on all of this.

I was a jumble of fatigue and elation, overwhelmed by each new wave of emotion and yet never wanting it to end. I was officially an Author. It still didn't feel real.

"Shall we go do something to celebrate?" I asked Dom. I'd had more than four decades of imagining what a book launch looked like, and none of my fantasies had ever included me practically horizontal on the couch.

Dom looked over to me with a sheepish look on his face. "Honestly? I'm knackered."

We stared at each other for a second, letting that sink in, before we both cracked up laughing. The reality may have been way less glamorous and more ridiculous than anything my imagination had ever come up with, but I knew we could both feel it. We were exactly where we were supposed to be.

Dom and I were clearing away our breakfast dishes on Friday morning when our intercom buzzed. I was always guaranteed to jump a mile whenever that thing buzzed, which usually sent Dom into a spiral of laughter, but this time we both froze like a couple of frightened rabbits. We darted our eyes toward each other.

"I'll go," Dom said. There was a weird ringing in my ears. I watched him talk into the intercom and then close the front door behind him. It took an ice age for him to come back, and all the while I attempted to breathe normally.

"Got it!" he sang out, marching back through the front door, a man on a mission. I let out a small squeak of anticipation as he deftly ripped the package open.

We'd officially announced and launched the book into the world, and yet, nothing could have prepared me for this moment. As Dom handed it over to me, tears flooded my eyes. I was holding the very first paperback copy in my hot little hands.

I thought about a wellness event I'd been to recently. During the Q&A session, a beautiful soul stood up and bravely shared the dream she had in her heart. Without skipping a beat, she then listed all the reasons she hadn't started yet, and all the people she believed she had to get approval from first. As though she needed all those ducks in a row before she could take action. Like she was waiting for someone to grant her permission to take the first step in doing something she loved.

And hadn't I always done exactly that? I could always come up with a ton of reasons why it wasn't a good time; why it was too hard; why I didn't know enough yet; why it had to happen later. But the truth was, just like sobriety, no one was coming to do the work for me. No one may have ever granted me permission. Creating a life I loved meant taking sole responsibility for the millions of tiny decisions I made every single day.

I shook my head tearfully. "Oh my God, I was so worried that it wouldn't arrive before the weekend, and now here it is. It's here! It's real. It's a *real book!*"

"And that's not all!" Dom said, raising his eyebrows and giving me a look that said, *I know something you don't know.*

I giggled, delighted. "What? What is it?"

He smiled, handing his phone to me so I could see for myself. "Congratulations, Bestseller!"

I stared at the screen, awestruck by the little "#1 Best Seller" flag next to our ebook version. "I can't believe it," I breathed. "No way!"

"Yes way!" Dom laughed, taking the phone back off me. "In multiple categories too."

I looked up to the heavens as if to say, 'Thank you, Universe' and spotted the clock. "*Eeep!* I've gotta run. But take a screenshot for me? I want to share it on social media later and say thank you. I'll share a photo of this baby too," I said, still grinning and waving the paperback in the air.

"Sure thing," he said, holding up his phone. "Say Cheese!"

I laughed and jumped in front of our bookcase so he could take a quick snap of me holding the magical first copy.

"Okay, I've gotta go!" I said, leaning in to hug him before grabbing my bag and rushing out the door.

Jenna and I had plans to meet for lunch at another of our favourite cafes in the city. I arrived just in time to save us a great table in the sunshine, and tried not to burst with excitement as I waited for her. My brain was buzzing with the power of a thousand bees.

I spotted Jenna and jumped up to hug hello, almost squishing the air out of her in my excitement.

"Congratulations, honey!" she laughed. "You did it!"

I beamed at her, unable to wipe the goofy grin from my face. "Thank you so much! The American copy arrived this morning, and holy moly, it still doesn't feel real…"

"I bet!" Jenna laughed. "Such a mammoth project. Remember when you thought you'd write it over the Christmas holidays?"

I covered my eyes with my hands, shaking my head at the madness of it all before dissolving into laughter with her. "Oh bless, I was so naïve."

"So what are you doing to celebrate?"

"Well, we're still a bit exhausted, so… *this*." I waved my arms around to indicate the cafe around us. My introverted heart was bursting at the thought of many more of these little lunches with friends and family over the coming weeks. "Plus we were thinking of hosting a movie night with the mocktail recipes I created for the book bonus."

I waited for her to tell me that was lame; that I should be doing something bigger and bolder and more extravagant, but instead her eyes searched my face and she smiled. "Sounds perfect."

I thought so too.

I'd planned to catch the city-link bus home after hugging Jenna goodbye, but changed my mind. I was still a bundle of nervous energy. Choosing a steep road with a hill that was practically vertical, I skipped all the way home.

Dom was creating graphics for the launch when I arrived. I collapsed onto the couch to catch my breath, worn out by the spontaneous climb.

The intercom buzzed a second after I'd finished sharing the surreal 'bestseller' news on social media.

"I'll get it!" I sang out to Dom, jumping up and performing a weird little dance number on my way out the door. I was humming at a volume that bordered on singing as I travelled down in the lift to collect it.

This was it; the last piece of the puzzle. The Australian proof copy. I beamed as I met the courier at the front entrance, barely stopping myself from hugging him, before dancing all the way back up and into our apartment.

"It's *heeeeere!*" I called out as I shimmied through

the front door, giggling in anticipation. I handed the package to Dom and headed back to reacquaint myself with the couch.

It was finally here. All those months of stress and worry that we wouldn't have books in time for the event melted from my shoulders and I felt giddy with relief.

Dom retrieved the box cutter from the middle drawer and carefully sliced the package open. I waited for his laugh, or some kind of grand gesture as he pulled it out of the package, or one of the silly comments he always made when he was truly happy.

"Oh," he said finally.

Coldness enveloped my entire body. "Oh?" I repeated. "What?"

"Something's not right," he said, handing the copy to me.

To my dismay, I saw what he meant. The front cover was all mottled and patchy where it should have been a uniform inky blue. The matte finish also felt super gummy, almost as though it had been laminated with jelly.

I stared at it, unable to comprehend how this could happen. I turned the book over in my hands. The back cover was just as weird and messed up as the front. "Good *grief!*"

It was always the Australian copies we'd planned to take to the event. Shipping a box of books from the US was horrendously expensive and painstakingly slow. Even if we could somehow find a way to pay for them, there was every possibility that they might not even arrive in time.

"I'll be honest," Dom said, reading my mind. "I'd be embarrassed to show up to the event with copies like this."

"We can't," I said, shaking my head. "If they all look like this… I mean, they'd be awful. They'd look ridiculous. I can't face people with these. What the hell do we do now?"

SIXTEEN

With a two-hour time difference between us and the east coast, by the time we contacted the Australian printer on Friday afternoon, their office was closed.

The weekend stretched out for a lifetime. We painfully tried to relax and distract ourselves with a movie marathon, while we desperately tried not to freak out.

It was almost lunchtime on Monday before we finally heard back. The representative seemed just as surprised by the issue as we were and advised that she would order a new, internal review copy, and get back to us when she had more news.

I read the email aloud to Dom. He closed his

eyes and sighed. "Okay, well we can't just sit around waiting. Time's running out. If we need to ship copies from the U.S., we need to make a decision, and *fast*. In the meantime, I've made an appointment with a local commercial printer. Let's go see what other options we have."

Surprised and a little excited by the unexpected field trip, I grabbed my coat. On the drive over, Dom told me he'd found this printer online and that they had experience with various projects, including creating books for local authors. They were located in an old, industrial part of the outer city.

Slowly driving past long-forgotten businesses and abandoned workshops, we'd barely managed to park the car before the heavens opened up. Dom unbuckled his seatbelt and reached into the backseat to find our umbrella, while I prayed this wasn't an omen.

Huddled together under our comically small weather shield, we ran up the path to the front entrance. Pushing open a small, unassuming door, we walked up a staircase into a surprisingly elegant reception area. Floor to ceiling glass overlooked half a dozen industrial printing presses on the factory floor. It looked to be quite the operation, and I felt my spirits lift.

"Hello," Dom said to the receptionist at the front desk, giving her our details, while I attempted to close our umbrella without spraying water all over the plush carpeting.

"He'll be with you in a moment," the receptionist smiled. "Please take a seat." She gestured to a large, open waiting area. As we wandered over, I was thrilled to see that the hardcover books and magazines spread out on the coffee tables were, in fact, printed by this very company.

On a table nearby was a flyer. Picking it up, I saw it was an invitation to a book launch for a local author. I ran my fingers over the details, wondering if this was the author's first book or launch party. I pictured people in tweed jackets with leather elbow patches, nodding as they chewed thoughtfully on their reading glasses, contemplating the overarching themes and 'true meaning of this *fine* piece of work'.

My reverie was interrupted by a man wearing a brown suit and a professional demeanour. "Dominic? Rebecca? Hi, I'm Alex. Come on through."

We stood and followed him. The windows behind his desk had a perfect view down to the printing presses below and I imagined how marvellous it would be to watch books being printed all day long.

Closing the office door behind us, he got down straight to business. "How can I help?"

Dom shared our predicament. "So we're in a bit of a pickle," he concluded. "Because we've committed to a book signing that's fast approaching and we don't have any books."

"Okay," Alex said, leaning back in his chair as he mulled this over. "The first thing you should know is that we print on very different presses to the global printing companies, and on very different paper.

We tend to focus on glossy magazines and illustrated books, rather than paperbacks."

Reaching over, he pulled something from the filing cabinet next to his desk. "Here, you can get an idea of what our stock is like." He handed the sheet to Dom, who in turn handed it to me. The paper was thick and smooth and lovely, just like in a glossy magazine or coffee table book, and not at all like the paper in a paperback.

"Oh," I said, crestfallen. "Could you print on different paper by any chance?"

"I'm afraid not." He shook his head. "Our presses are only compatible with this type of paper. We could still print on this to create paperbacks, but the cost might be more than you're expecting." He paused. "Why don't I draw up a quote, and then we can see if it works for you?"

"That'd be great," I said. "Thank you."

"No problem," he said, standing up. "I'll get it to you by close of business tomorrow."

It was only after we'd shaken hands and headed out the doors that I realised exactly what this would mean: more waiting.

"So," I said, making a sound that was somewhere between a groan and a giggle as we sidestepped the rain on the way to our car. "Do we have a Plan C?"

We tried not to watch the clock as we waited for answers from the printers, but every hour was excruciating. Once again, we busied ourselves in work. I really didn't want to face the fact that another day had passed us by and we were still no closer to having a solution.

Finally, that afternoon, I received an email from the Australian distributor on the east coast.

"Email! Email!" I yelped, running into the living room so I could read it aloud to Dom. I made sure he was listening before clicking it open. "Hi Rebecca, I have received the internal copy and I'm sorry to say it is exactly the same as the version you have received. It is a different blue. I have attached an image."

I tried not to let disappointment drown me as I opened the attachment and zoomed in on the image.

Were my eyes playing tricks on me?

"I'm not sure…" I said. "But I think this one actually looks okay?" I handed the phone to Dom so he could see for himself.

He turned the phone in a circle, slowly inspecting the image from all angles. "It's hard to tell from this photo, but… it just might be. Maybe ask her to courier that copy to us so we can see it in person?"

"Roger that," I nodded, striding back to my laptop. "Plan A is still in motion!"

I'd only just finished sending off the email when Dom hollered out from the living room. "The quote's here!"

I ran out to find him peering at his computer

screen. "From the local printer?"

"Yep," he said, his nose still pressed up against the glass. Finally, he let out a heavy sigh.

My heart sank. "No good?"

"Plan B's out," he confirmed. "The cost per copy is way too high. The books would be too expensive."

"Okay," I nodded. "Let me think. There's a chance that the Australian distributor's proof copy will be fine, and then we can still put our order through there as we'd planned all along. If we pay express shipping for the large order, it should - hopefully - arrive in time." I ran my fingers through my hair, trying to think. "Plan C… *hhhmmm*… shall we run the numbers on trying to ship from the U.S. again? Just in case?"

"Let's do it," Dom nodded, opening a calendar on his computer. "We'll need to check the dates too; see if it's even possible to get them here that quickly."

"Fingers crossed," I said, sending a mental S.O.S. out to the Universe as I frantically crunched the figures one more time.

SEVENTEEN

When the Australian distributor's proof still hadn't arrived three days later, we were beside ourselves. It was Friday and there would be no more courier deliveries until Monday. This was it. The gig was up.

The U.S. copies were almost as expensive as the local printer, but we might *just* be able to receive them in time if we ordered by that very afternoon.

I felt like climbing the walls. I was desperate to get out of the apartment; to go for one of our stress-busting walks in the park, but we were too scared to leave, worried that if we left for even five minutes, we might miss the courier.

We even took bathroom breaks in shifts, ensuring that one person's ear was firmly on the intercom at all times. I couldn't stop myself from checking and rechecking the volume on the buzzer all morning, willing the delivery to *please, for the love of God,* arrive today.

Finally, around 2:00pm, the intercom buzzed and I almost peed my pants in nervous anticipation.

"You go!" I mouthed the words to Dom, terrified to speak in case I somehow scared the delivery away and woke up to find this was all a dream. I tip-toed over to the couch and sat down, ready to stoically await the news.

Dom reentered the apartment in silence and headed straight to the kitchen drawer to retrieve the box cutter. I noticed his hands were shaking as he sliced the package open and pulled out the book.

"I think…" he said after a moment, turning the copy over in his hands. "It's fine."

I jumped to my feet so I could see it for myself. "It is?" I yelped. "It is!" Overjoyed with relief, I fell about laughing, before jumping up and down like a three-year-old. "It's really, really fine and normal!"

Dom picked me up and spun me around, joining in my laughter. "Okay, quick!" he said, suddenly putting me down. "Let's place the order before they close for the weekend."

The order form was already open on my laptop. I ran to it. With a click I submitted the order for one hundred books, paying extra for express shipping, and once again feeling immense gratitude for my parents' generous gift. I prayed this copy wasn't a fluke. We didn't have anything in our budget for a second batch of books; everything we had was riding on this one.

I sent an email to the representative thanking her profusely for her help and letting her know that the proof copy was fine.

Once again we could only cross our fingers and wait, hoping against hope that the ordered batch would be perfectly fine and normal like the copy we'd just received.

~

I tried not to go completely mental while we waited, busying ourselves with getting everything else ready for the event. My mood swung wildly between feeling incredibly optimistic and freaking out that it was too late for any other options to be open to us.

Six of the longest days on earth passed before I was finally put out of my misery. That Thursday afternoon, the intercom buzzed. I let out a strangled yelp of excitement in Dom's general direction. "Let's both go."

Grabbing our keys, we travelled down in the lift in silence, not wanting to say or do anything that might possibly jinx it. We did our best impression of being sane, normal human beings as we signed for the three boxes, and thanked the courier.

My head was spinning as we carried them back up to the apartment. *This was it!*

In the living room, I worried that I might throw up as Dom placed the first box onto the kitchen counter and delicately sliced it open.

"Please let them be okay," I mumbled, crossing my fingers. "*Please please please.*"

I held my breath as Dom started digging down through the packing peanuts in the box, spilling them all over the floor. He paused as he reached the books inside and I thought I'd burst with suspense.

I closed my eyes. I couldn't look.

"Hey *hey*," Dom laughed, holding two books up for me to see as I opened my eyes. "They're great!"

I squealed with delight, almost floored by the rush of excitement, relief and happiness. "All the way down?" I asked, reaching over to pull more books out, and feeling giddy with gratitude as each one was as lovely as the next.

"Let's take them all out," Dom said flashing me a wicked grin and those dimples I loved so much. "I want to see them all lined up along the floor. I want to see what one hundred of our books looks like."

I giggled and nodded, in love with the idea.

When we'd finally unpacked them all, taken a million photos, and reassured ourselves over and over that this wasn't a dream, we packed them back into the boxes again, wanting to keep them pristine for the event.

I couldn't wait to greet all the beautiful souls at the event and give them a signed copy.

"What kind of pen should I take?" I wondered

aloud to Dom. "Or maybe a coloured marker?"

Suddenly the thought of defacing a book, any book - especially *my* book - had me in a mild panic. I'd never written in a book before, not even in textbooks.

Wide-eyed, I spun around to face Dom, "What do I write in the books?"

He gave me a strange look. "What do you mean? It's already written."

"No, when I sign it. Do I write *their* name? Do I write *my* name? Like, with a heart or something?"

Dom laughed. "Write whatever you like."

I paused, contemplating my options.

"I think I need to go practice my signature," I said, scrambling back to my office.

~

I'd always admired those effortlessly graceful and lithe people, from my place amongst the chronically awkward and clumsy. The next day, exhausted and desperate to finish my presentation now that the books were safely in our possession, I rushed past the spare chair in my office. Miscalculating the distance, I rammed the thin, metal chair leg directly between the two smallest toes on my left foot. A colossal thunderbolt of pain cracked through me. Shocked and confused, I screamed in agony and fell to the floor.

"What happened!" Dom called as he came running from the living room.

"*Oww! Fuuuuuuuck! Owww!*" I gasped and spluttered, shocked by the intense pain. "Toe! Banged. Off! Sock."

"What?" he said.

I tried again, spinning my arms around wildly as I alternated between sobbing and taking huge, heaving breaths. "Rushed. Chair. Banged. Toe. Off! In sock."

To my utter surprise, Dom laughed. "It hasn't come off, silly. If it had come off, there'd be blood everywhere. Here, let me see."

Slightly indignant at his response, I cautiously inched my foot toward him, tears still streaming down my face. I craned my neck so I could watch as he removed my sock, mentally preparing myself for what I might be about to see. This could be it. *Goodbye, sweet toe. I'll miss you.*

"There," Dom said, as he carefully removed the last of the sock. "Still intact."

He was right. My toes were angrily pulsating and as shockingly red as they felt, but I was all still very much in one piece.

As Dom let go of my foot, I continued rocking my body back and forth, demanding the pain to subside. "Good," I mumbled, wiping away tears.

"I think you should go to the Doctor though," Dom said, standing up.

"*Noooo,*" I moaned, shaking my head in complete protest. He *knew* I had a huge case of White Coat Syndrome and yet he was continuously trying to get me there.

"*Yes,*" Dom insisted. "If it hurts this much, it's

probably broken."

"Huh?" I'd never broken a bone in my life, but I couldn't remind him of that now. There was still far too much pain to allow for complete sentences. "Not. Broken. Sprained. Banged. Jus' hurts. And owwww…" I groaned and writhed in agony as another wave of pain crashed over my foot.

"I'm making an appointment for you," Dom said, striding out to retrieve his phone from the kitchen before returning. "If you won't go to the Doctor, you can at least go to the Physio to get it checked out."

Was he for real? We didn't have time for that; we had an event to prepare for. Besides, what if the white coats *did* say it was broken? I couldn't exactly get up onto the stage in crutches. Were we just going to give up on our plan?

Still winded and nauseated from the pain, I struggled to my feet and hobbled over to pull his phone from him. "All fine," I whispered. "Be okay."

I made it the two steps to my desk chair and collapsed into it, commanding the blood that was pounding from my foot to my brain to calm the heck down. I hadn't come this far to be stopped by a little toe, for crying out loud. I wasn't going to be stopped now.

EIGHTEEN

The morning of the event dawned cold and sunny. Dom and I rushed around the apartment, packing up the myriad of things we needed to take with us.

"Okay I've got the sign, the books, the camera…" Dom said, counting them off on his fingers as he checked each item. I wasn't due on stage until 12:45pm but doors opened at 11:00am and we needed to have our stall completely set up by then.

Part of me was beyond excited to actually be doing my very first book signing. The other part of me was terrified. We'd invited some friends and family to come along and I was hoping some friendly faces would help dispel my nerves. My hands were still shaking as I read over my presentation notes for the millionth time.

Loaded up with all our stuff, we piled into a cab, asking the driver to drop us off as close to the venue as possible.

"How's your toe?" Dom whispered, reaching across the back seat to squeeze my hand.

"It's okay," I shrugged. I'd secured it firmly inside a tight-fitting sock and my flat, knee-high boots. Despite taking painkillers, it still throbbed whenever I moved, but I figured the speaking jitters and adrenaline would soon take over. It would be another two days before I'd go for the x-ray that would confirm it was fractured. For now I'd chosen to believe that it was perfectly fine, and could only hope that no one would accidentally step on it.

Trekking like sherpas across the street and up the stairs with all our gear, we arrived to find the main hall in a flurry of activity. Dozens of people rushed about, busily setting up their stalls.

Sasha bustled past us carrying a clipboard. "Oh hi, guys!" she called out, barely slowing down, pointing at a table nearby. "That stall over there is yours. Just come find me if you have any problems." With a wave, she disappeared around the corner.

We shuffled over to unload our supplies. While I started unpacking the books, Dom got to work hoisting our giant poster up onto its stand. It was a massive picture of me with the book, which made me feel both euphoric and squeamish at the same time.

"There we go," Dom said, adjusting the last clip into place. "Lucky there's no breeze in here or it might set sail!" he joked, and I loved him for making me laugh.

Just then Ben walked in carrying all of his camera equipment and a huge smile. "Hey guys, I'll take some photos around the venue first, and then head upstairs to see if I can get some cool shots of the stage."

We'd just finished thanking him and unpacking another box of books when the main hall began to flood with people. The doors downstairs had officially opened to the public.

"Hi Bex!" a woman said, appearing in front of me. "I love your blog and I'm so excited to read your book. Can you sign it to Leslie please?"

"Absolutely, Leslie," I beamed, struggling to believe this was real life. My hand was shaking as I lifted a copy from the top of the pile and opened the front cover. The entire moment had a surreal quality to it, almost like it was happening in slow motion or I was having an out-of-body experience. With an attempt at a flourish, I signed the book with her name, my signature, *and* a heart, just like I'd practiced.

I handed it to her and watched in awe as she smiled and walked away. My first book signed. My first in-person meeting with a real, live reader.

A warm, gooey feeling overwhelmed me and I was a split-second from erupting into happy, messy tears when more people appeared in front of me.

"Hi!" I smiled, just barely piecing it back together. Each person was just as lovely as the next and I had a ton of fun meeting them and signing their books.

By the time my parents arrived, I was starving, but Dom and I were far too busy to forage for food from one of the many stalls downstairs.

"Have you eaten?" Mum said. "We'll go get you some food."

"Thank you!" I called after them, counting my lucky stars for beautiful Mums who could read minds, and hoping that I wouldn't be too overcome with nerves to actually eat it.

My sister and her family arrived next, along with Dom's Mum and a few of our friends, and I felt myself getting all emotional all over again. It meant the world to me to have them there to support us.

We'd only just hugged them all hello when my parents returned. "Huge queues down there and we knew you didn't have much time, so we grabbed what we could," Mum said, passing us a few paper bags filled with sugary cakes, as well as a fluffy pink bliss ball the size of a cat's head.

"Amazing, thank you!" I said, hugging her again. I wasn't sure if it was such a hot idea to stuff my face with sugar right before my talk but I figured a sugar high beat the loss of brain power and vocabulary I experienced whenever I was hungry.

Choosing one bag and handing the rest to Dom, I scurried over to a quiet corner out in the corridor, away from view. I was a jumble of sweat, nerves, hunger, and adrenalin. On the bright side, this ridiculous blend had worked wonders in overriding the pain in my toe. Scoffing the cake down in three bites, I hurried back to help Dom.

Our stall faced away from the main stage and I kept busy, not wanting to watch the other speakers this time. Trying to stay calm as more people approached our stand. I didn't want to think about my talk at all.

The stall next to us belonged to some sort of vegan superstar. People of all ages swarmed his stall, buying his t-shirts and putting them straight on. Young women crowded him, gushing as they told him their stories, and posing for photos.

I checked the time on my phone. "I'd better go," I told Dom. "I'm on in ten minutes."

"Okay, I'll keep manning the booth while you're up there," he said, leaning over to hug me. "Good luck, sweetie!"

I tried to slow my breathing as I walked past the rows of seats, up the stairs at the side of the stage, and into the wings. *Remember how well it went last time,* I told myself. *You've got this.*

The man who was presenting before me was still on stage. He was a doctor, and clearly a seasoned speaker. He completely commanded the stage; confidence oozing out of him. I peeked out towards the audience. They were totally eating it up. There's no way I could follow this guy. What the hell was I doing here?

I looked down at my toe and briefly wondered how far I'd get if I made a run for it.

It's just your first time with a crowd this size, I reminded myself. *You get points simply for trying.*

Applause rang out across the hall and the man came off stage looking completely relaxed and happy with himself.

A woman appeared carrying a clipboard. "Okay, you're up," she pointed at me before walking backstage.

Blood pounded in my ears as I shuffled my way towards the podium. I could clearly see our book signing stand from the stage. Dom was struggling to point the camera over the crowd, trying to film me while also chatting with people and handing over books. I could just make out Ben in the rafters, his camera lens aimed straight at me.

In direct contrast to the dark, intimate nightclub of my last talk, this place was huge and brightly lit. Stalls lined the back of the room, and people continued to drift in and out of the hall, some taking seats to look through their purchases and then jumping back up again; others continuing to chat and laugh as they moved around the stalls.

I swallowed hard. Why the hell had I agreed to this? My brain short-circuited and blew a fuse, hopped-up on sugar and struggling to remember how on earth I did this the last time.

I cleared my throat. *Find friendly faces and focus on those,* a little voice inside my head whispered. Oh yeah.

Scanning the audience, I spotted our friends and family sitting together in about the tenth row and felt marginally better.

With a deep, trembling breath, I began.

My voice sounded small and inconsequential in the booming, cavernous space. Whereas last time I'd felt the crowd connecting to me and my words, this time most people were distracted or disinterested, which only made my nerves and delivery worse.

Just keep going, I told myself, continuing to bring my focus back to the faces of my family and friends in the first few rows. *Give it all you've got.*

Twenty minutes later, I finally finished, my conclusion met with a tiny, polite round of applause. By all accounts, it was definitely not my finest hour. But strangely, as I left the stage, I wasn't crushed.

In fact, as I hobbled back to our stall, I felt peculiar, in a way I couldn't quite describe.

I could see a small crowd of beautiful souls gathered around our stall, books in hand, waiting for me to sign them.

My book. My readers. My lifelong dream.

And suddenly I realised that it had been about this all along. It had never really been about my goal or dream; it had been about how the process of going after something I'd previously believed impossible would *change* me. It was about who I needed to *become* in order to realise my dream.

Anything worthwhile in life took grit, gumption,

and so much more time than we imagined. It was so tempting to want to fast forward; to skip over all the messy, painful parts and get to the good stuff. But it was this slow, beautiful journey that changed us on the deepest level.

Every challenging moment - every time we felt like we were moving two steps forward and one step back - we were learning, growing, and becoming all we are meant to be.

By the time I reached Dom, my eyes had filled with tears.

"You did it!" he laughed, pulling me into a hug.

"I did it," I nodded, laughing and crying at the same time, almost collapsing into him. Past his shoulder I could see several faces smiling at me, and I pulled myself together. Wiping away tears, I turned, ready to meet more readers and sign more books.

LOVE NOTE

In the process of writing this book, I thought a lot about courage, perseverance, and overcoming our own limiting beliefs.

Your hopes and desires don't have to be anything like mine. Whether your biggest, boldest dream has always been to write a book, play in a band, teach a class, or climb a mountain, I wrote this book to encourage you to *try*. And not just try for the little dreams, but for the big dreams too.

Maybe it'll work out, and maybe it won't, but one thing's for sure: the experience itself will change you to your very core. It'll make you stronger and more resilient. It'll lift you up, and teach you more than you could ever imagine about who you are and who you were always meant to be.

And decades from now, when you're cosy in your bed, you'll be able to look back with a twinkle in your eye and say, "I *did* that".

With love,
Bex

ALSO BY REBECCA WELLER

A HAPPIER HOUR

When Rebecca Weller's pounding, dehydrated head woke her at 3am, yet again, she stared at the ceiling, wondering why the hell she kept doing this to herself. At 39 years of age - and a Health Coach, no less - she knew better than to down several bottles of wine per week. Her increasingly dysfunctional relationship with alcohol had to stop, but after decades of social drinking, she was terrified of what that might mean.

How could she live a joyful existence, without alcohol? How would she relax, socialise, or celebrate - without wine?

In sheer frustration, on a morning filled with regret and tears, she embarks on a 3-month sobriety experiment that becomes a quest for self-discovery, and ultimately, transforms her entire world.

A Happier Hour is a heartfelt, moving, and inspiring story for anyone who has ever had to give up something they loved in order to get what they truly wanted.

ABOUT THE AUTHOR

Rebecca Weller is a coach, writer, and speaker. Named 'one of Perth's leading Health-preneurs' by The Sunday Times Magazine, Rebecca helps women from around the world to get their sparkle back and create a life they love.

Author of the bestselling memoir, *A Happier Hour*, and the long-awaited follow-up, *Up All Day*, Rebecca writes about love, life, and the strength and potential of the human spirit.

Her work has been featured by the Telstra Business Awards, The Australian, The Huffington Post, MindBodyGreen, Fast Company, Good Health Magazine, Marie Claire Australia, and Elle Quebec.

She lives in sunny Perth, Western Australia, with her husband, Dominic.

Learn more, plus receive a weekly love note full of inspiration and special book bonus gifts, at
BexWeller.com.

Manufactured by Amazon.ca
Bolton, ON

27399036R00122